Dreams: Where do Biblical, Zambian, and Western Approaches
Meet?

DREAMS

Where do Biblical, Zambian, and Western Approaches Meet?

Gotthard Rosner, Bernhard Udelhoven, Patrick Mumbi

Published in Zambia by FENZA

(Faith and Encounter Centre Zambia), Lusaka

ISBN: 978-9982-22-675-2

Imprint (for international distribution):

CreateSpace Independent Publishing Platform

ISBN-13: 978-1482398953

ISBN-10: 1482398958

Distributed by CreateSpace

February 2013

Dreams: Where do Biblical, Zambian, and Western Approaches Meet?

Authors: Gotthard Rosner, Bernhard Udelhoven and Patrick Mumbi

Copyright © 2013 Faith and Encounter Centre Zambia (FENZA)

Published in Zambia by FENZA
(Faith and Encounter Centre Zambia)
P.O. Box 320 076
Lusaka
Zambia
Email: director@fenza.org
ISBN: 978-9982-22-675-2
Publishing date (edition printed in Zambia): January 2013

Published for international distribution by CreateSpace Independent Publishing Platform
ISBN-13: 978-1482398953
ISBN-10: 1482398958
Distributed by CreateSpace

Publication date (edition printed for international distribution): February 2013

FENZA Publications

The Faith and Encounter Centre Zambia (FENZA) was founded in 2007 as an initiative of the Missionaries of Africa, with the aim of empowering Christians in Zambia to face in openness the challenges of contemporary and traditional cultures, and to encounter people of different Christian denominations, contemporary religious movements and religions.

FENZA publishes documents and organises conferences to facilitate discussions on issues that touch the Christian faith in Zambia. For other FENZA publications you may consult the FENZA website (www.fenza.org).

Table of contents

Preface

What does the Bible say about dreams? What do Zambian cultures say? And how does this all mix with Western psychology? Dreams are important in Zambia. Yet when Christians try to find meaning in their dreams, they have to juggle with very different worldviews.

This book identifies and clarifies some important issues when looking at dreams in Zambia's multicultural context. It is written for all who have an interest in dreams, from the perspectives of Zambian cultural traditions, psychology and theology. It is of special benefit for those who help people in the pastoral field to deal with compelling dream experiences.

The articles in this book are based on presentations made during two FENZA conferences on dreams in Zambia. The first conference was organised back in 2011; the interested audience showed us that we were dealing with a very important topic. We organised a follow-up conference in 2012. Here about a hundred people participated from very different walks of life, including a number of traditional healers, people trained in Western psychology, Biblicists and pastors from different Churches. Many people attending the conferences were seeking answers to their own dreams. It was clear that the discussions on dreams in a multicultural context had only just started; we decided to publish our different contributions in this booklet to allow for the discussions to continue, hopefully on a broader level.

FENZA conferences bring together people of various educational backgrounds. Also for this book we hope for a wide and diverse readership. Since we are aware that not every reader is accustomed to all academic words that are used in this book, we have included a glossary (wordlist) of academic terms; some readers may benefit from consulting it when unsure about the meaning of a specific word.

We thank all persons who participated in our discussions and who have helped in writing this book. ZIKOMO. The FENZA Team

PREFACE

Glossary

Anthropology	The "science of humanity" which deals, often through cross-cultural comparison, with the study of human societies, relationships among individuals and groups, and the ways in which people make sense of the world around them. It is related to Sociology.[1]
Carthage	Influential ancient town in Tunisia (today's Tunis).
Church Fathers	Early, influential theologians and eminent Christian teachers, often bishops. Their scholarly works were used as a precedent for centuries to come.[1]
Cibanda	(Bemba), *ciwanda* (Nyanja): the shade, spiritual presence, or soul of a dead person, usually not of one's own kin, that sticks to an unfortunate person as a negative influence. In many Zambian cultural traditions, a widower or widow needs to be cleansed of the *cibanda* of the late spouse to be enabled to remarry outside the late spouse's family.
Cognitive psychology	A psychological approach investigating internal mental processes: how people perceive, think, remember, or solve problems.1
Desert Fathers	Hermits, ascetics, and monks who lived mainly in the deserts around the Holy Land and Egypt beginning the third century after Christ. Saint Anthony the Great is one of the best known Desert Fathers.[1]
Divine dreams	Dreams inspired by God.
Enlightenment	In this book the term refers to the European intellectual movement known as the Age of Enlightenment, also called the Age of Reason, based on philosophical developments related to scientific

---

[1] Taken and adapted from Wikipedia (en.wikipedia.org)

	rationality in the 17th and 18th centuries and marked by radical questioning of all belief systems and a search for objective truths.[1]
Gladiator	An armed fighter who entertained audiences in the Roman Empire in violent confrontations with other gladiators, wild animals or condemned criminals.[1]
Introspection	The self-examination of one's conscious thoughts and feelings.[1]
Irrational	Action or opinions are described as irrational when they are seen to be given through inadequate use of reason, emotional distress, or cognitive deficiency. The term is used, usually pejoratively, to describe thinking and actions that are, or appear to be, less useful, or more illogical than other more rational alternatives.[1]
Magisterium	Teaching office of the Catholic Church
Mashawe	(Nyanja). Bemba: *ngulu*. Possessing spirits, related to the land (or to past or foreign peoples) that initially bring sickness to the person they possess (physically and/or mentally) but that may also bestow on the person special spiritual abilities if appeased.
Medieval	The Middle Ages (adjectival form: medieval) is a name given to the period of European history roughly between the 5th to the 15th centuries after Christ. Usually the Middle Ages are seen to start after the collapse of the Western Roman Empire (the end of Classical Antiquity) and to end with the Renaissance and the Age of Discovery, which are the periods giving birth to the Modern Era.[1]
Monastic Theology	Theology that developed in the schools of monks and monasteries during Medieval times.
Mupashi	(Bemba), *mzimu* (Nyanja): the soul or spirit of the departed, often of one's own kin. The term also refers to other spiritual realities, for example one's own soul.
Mystic	A person living a reflective life out of his/her own

personal experiences with God.

Neo-Platonism | A school of mystical philosophy that took shape in the 3rd century after Christ, based on the teachings of Plato (who himself was teaching in the 4th century before Christ).[1]

Neurobiology | The scientific study of the nervous system.[1]

Neuron | A nerve cell.

Ng'anga | Traditional healer.

Ngulu | (Bemba). See *Mashawe*

Paradigm | A set of practices, concepts, models and patterns that determine a scientific discipline or outlook during a particular period of time. Paradigms change throughout history, leading to major general shifts in worldviews and outlooks.[1]

Patristic times | Early Christian times of the Church Fathers (see above).

Postmodern theories | While modern theories rely heavily on scientific or objective efforts to explain reality, postmodern theories challenge the assumption that reality is mirrored in human understanding of it. Apparent realities are but social constructs, formed by language and concepts and sustained through human practices; explanations are only interpretations seen from a specific viewpoint. In the social sciences postmodern theories are sceptical of explanations that claim to be valid for all groups, cultures or traditions, and instead focus on relative truths and their presuppositions. Postmodern theories also are interested in the relationship between power and socially constructed knowledge.[1]

Prayer guides | A group of Christian (Catholic) counsellors in Lusaka Archdiocese who receive a wide range of training programmes that enable them to guide people through individual guided retreats and help them connect their spirituality with the challenges of daily life.

GLOSSARY

Preconscious	Freud described thoughts or affects as preconscious when they are unconscious at the particular moment in question, but not repressed and therefore in principle available for recall and capable of becoming conscious.[1]
Presuppositions	Assumptions about the world (usually preconscious) that make possible a certain way of thought and reasoning.
Psychoanalysis	A school of thought that tries to make conscious the unconscious human drives that are blocked out from awareness through elaborate defence mechanisms, often developed during early childhood, that influence individual personality formation and coping mechanisms and may contribute towards mental sickness, neurotic traits or anxieties and depressions.[1]
Psychodynamic theories	Theory and systematic study of the internal psychological forces that underlie human behaviour.[1]
Psychology	The study of the mind and mental functions.
Psychotherapy	Refers in a wide sense to therapeutic interaction between a trained professional and a patient (or a family, couple, or group) to address psychological issues, increase the person's sense of well-being or help to design better ways of coping with difficult realities.[1]
Reductionism	Understanding the nature of complex realities by reducing them to the interactions of their parts, or to simpler or more fundamental realities. Religious reductionism for example attempts to explain religion or spiritual reality by boiling it down to certain nonreligious or nonspiritual causes.[1] God, spirits or demons are thought to be fully explained by making recourse to psychological, social or biological forces. Vice versa, to explain physical, biological, psychological or social issues solely with reference to spiritual forces is also a form of reductionism.
Reformation	The Protestant Reformation was the 16th century schism within Western Christianity initiated by

Martin Luther, John Calvin and other early Protestants.[1]

Repressed Sexuality   A state in which a person is prevented from expressing his/her sexuality. Sexual repression is often linked to feelings of guilt or shame being associated with sexual impulses. Sigmund Freud, who greatly shaped early modern psychology at the beginning of the 20th century, believed that people's naturally strong instincts toward sexuality were repressed in order to meet the constraints imposed on them by civilised social life. He saw in sexual repression the roots of many major problems of Western civilisation and tried to trace dream symbols to repressed sexual impulses.[1]

Schism   A split between people belonging to the same religion that establishes two separate groups, no longer in communion with each other.

Scholastic theology   A method of critical thought which dominated teaching by the academics (called "scholastics", or schoolmen) of medieval universities in Europe from about 1100–1500 CE.[1]

Social facts   Values, cultural norms, and social structures which transcend (go beyond) the individual and are capable of exercising a social constraint. The term was popularised in the field of Sociology by Émile Durkheim at the end of the 19th century.[1]

Sociology   The scientific study of human social behaviour and its origins, development, organisations and institutions.[1]

Spirituality   An inner path or method of developing one's inner life in view of finding God and living one's faith in daily life.

Synapse   A cell structure that permits a neuron (or nerve cell) to pass an electrical or chemical signal to another cell.[1] The human brain develops constantly new synapses and thereby establishes new routes for signals, thus constituting for example different types of memories and diverse "programmed" or automatized forms of responding to impulses from outer and inner realities.

Taboo

A fervent prohibition of an action based on the belief that such action is either too sacred or under a curse for ordinary individuals to undertake, under threat of supernatural punishment.[1]

Theology

"Faith seeking understanding": the systematic study of religion and of religious truths from the perspective of one's faith.

Transpersonal

In transpersonal experiences the sense of identity or self extends beyond (trans) the individual or personal to encompass wider aspects of humankind, life, psyche or cosmos.[1]

Unconscious

The processes in the mind that occur automatically and are not available to introspection, and include thought processes, memory, affect, and motivation.[1]

Worldview

The total framework of ideas and beliefs through which an individual, group or culture interprets the world and interacts with it.

1

Dreams in the Bible

Gotthard Rosner

Dreams, visions and experiences of the Spirit

The Bible knows of many dreams, visions, and appearances of angels and spiritual experiences which are regarded as messages coming from God. A dream is an experience which a person has during sleep i.e. during a naturally unconscious state. A vision, trance or spiritual experience happens in a semi-conscious state, when we are awake, but resembles a dream.

Some people believe that it is normal to have a dream, but that it is a sign of mental sickness to have a vision or trance. This, however, is not the case. If a vision is accepted as an external reality and seen as an objective truth, and if the consciousness does not distinguish between the external and interior world, then indeed we can speak of mental sickness. But if the person recognises the vision or trance as an interior happening belonging to the internal nature of a person, then this is a normal situation. The Bible knows dreams and visions and recognises in them a message of God.

In Numbers 12:6 we read: "Hear my words: If there is a prophet among you, I the Lord make myself known to him in a vision. I speak to him in a dream". Dreams and visions are considered coming from God. The Bible also equates the appearance of an angel with a dream or vision. Mt. 1:20 tells us that an angel appeared to Joseph in a dream telling him to take Mary as his wife and to assure him that the child was conceived by the Holy Spirit. See also Mt. 2:19; Lk. 1:22; 24:23; Acts 10:3; Rev. 9:17; etc.

The similarity of having a dream or vision and "being in the spirit" is shown several times in the book of Ezekiel: "the Spirit lifted me up between heaven and earth and brought me in a vision of God to Jerusalem..." (8:3; cf. 11:24, 40:2, etc.) The book of Joel is quoted in the Acts of the Apostles 2:17: "And in the last days it shall be, so speaks the Lord, that I will pour out my Spirit upon all flesh, and your sons and your daughters will prophesy, and your young men shall see visions, and your old men shall dream dreams".

We have indeed in the Bible a fine line between dreams, visions, appearances of angels and the outpouring of the Spirit of God (cf. 1 Sam. 3:1; 28:6; 1 Chron. 17:3; Hos. 12:10; Acts 9:10; 16:9; 18:9; etc.) It is clear that dreams, visions, trance and spiritual experiences were regarded as revelations from God and that they can be interchanged with one another.

Different kinds of dreams in the Bible

Job 33: 14-16: "For God may speak in one way or in another, yet man does not perceive it. In a dream, in a vision of the night, when deep sleep falls on men while slumbering on their beds, then he opens the ears of men and seals their instruction."

The dream in the Bible is a central form of the experience of God, and if a person does not listen to her/his dreams, she/he does not listen to God. We would expect that the text speaks of opening the eyes when seeing a dream, but it speaks of the ears. To have a dream and to interpret it is equal to listening to the word of God.

There are three different kinds of dreams in the Bible:

- There is the pure or direct dream. The images of the dream are clear and ask for an immediate action. The typical examples are the dreams of Joseph in the New Testament in Mt. Chapters 1-2.

- Then there are the allegorical dreams. Certain images and symbols are used and must be interpreted. Some are rather easy to interpret, but others are difficult. The best examples are the dreams of Joseph in the Old Testament. In Gen. 37:5-11 Joseph's brothers have no difficulty in understanding his dream.

- But in Gen. 40:1-23 the symbols are more difficult to interpret, and Joseph attributes his explanation to God himself. "Do not the interpretations of dream belong to God himself? Tell them to me please" (vs. 8). Joseph becomes an instrument of God to interpret dreams and by doing so he will save Israel.

Some allegories are rather extreme and need a special gift of interpretation like the fat and meagre cows or the good ears and withered ears of wheat in the dreams of Pharaoh (Gen. 41:1-7; 17-36).

The most difficult dreams in the Bible are called dreams of incubation. A person would like that God reveals the future to him and asks for a dream during the night. This wish is connected with prayer or a sacrifice. Solomon has to offer 1000 holocausts before God reveals himself in a dream and gives the king the gift of wisdom and discernment (1 Kings 3:4 ff.).

In Dan 2 we find the story of king Nebuchadnezzar who is afflicted by insomnia, but is aware of dreams which he cannot recall. Since he knows that these dreams were important, he calls the Babylonian "magoi" (English Magi) who are diviners, astrologers, magicians, witchdoctors. They are unable to help the king who decides to kill them all, if they would not reveal the dream to him in three days. Daniel is included in this group, but he and his companions pray to God, and accordingly the mystery was revealed to him in a dream (2:19). He confronts the king and says: "No wise men, enchanters, magicians or astrologers can show to the king the mystery which the king has asked, but there is a God in heaven who reveals mysteries and who shows king Nebuchadnezzar what will happen in the latter days. God has revealed this mystery to me in order that the interpretation may be known to the king, and that you may know the thoughts of your mind." (2:27-30)

This last phrase is especially significant to us, for it is exactly what the interpretation of a dream does for us: It reveals to us the thoughts of our unconscious mind. The word 'mind' can literally stand for the word 'heart'. It means the inmost person, the secret thoughts and deepest emotions". (Sanford, 1989, 90)

Critical voices in the Bible concerning dreams

It is astonishing that most of the dreams narrated in the Old Testament occur in the territory of foreign people: Egypt, Babylonia, Moab, Median, etc. The gift of interpreting dreams was known all over the ancient Middle East. The Bible, however, is carefully avoiding anything that could lead away from its strict Monotheism, the belief in one God.

Deut. 13:2-6 tells us: "If a prophet or a dreamer of dreams arises among you, offering you some sign or miracle... and if he says to you 'Let us follow other gods and serve them', you must not listen to that prophet's words or to that dreamer's dreams..." The criterion for the correctness of a dream is the fidelity to the God of the Covenant. Jeremiah attacks false prophets and false dreamers: "I have heard what the prophets say who speak lies in my name. I have had a dream, say say, I have had a dream... They are doing their best by means of the dreams to make my people forget my name... Let the prophet who has had a dream tell it for what it is, a dream" (Jer. 23:25-28). Ben Sira is even more outspoken: "Dreams are no different from mirrors, confronting a face, the reflection of that face. What can be cleansed by uncleanness, what can be verified by falsehood. Divinations, visions and dreams are nonsense, like the fantasies of a pregnant woman. Unless sent as a messenger from the Most High, do not give them a thought, for dreams have led many astray..." (Ecclesiasticus 34:3-8).

Dreams in the New Testament

The early Christians did believe in dreams, but took up a very critical attitude towards them. Except for Mt. 1-2 there is no central theme of the gospel being based on a dream revelation. Paul in his letters does never refer to any of the dreams mentioned in Acts. Yet these dreams were milestones in the life of the young Church: Peter in a trance is told to accept and baptize the Gentiles (Act. ch.10); Paul in a dream is told to cross over to Europe (Act. 16: 9-10); he is encouraged in founding the new community at Corinth (Act. 18:9) and is told that he will be Christ's witness in Rome (Act. 23:11; 27:23-24).

None of the dreams in the NT requires an interpretation by some-body else. They all are "direct dreams". All the New Testament dream narratives are centred on Jesus Christ and thus become revelation. God guides the young Church and encourages his disciples.

Conclusion

- The Bible speaks of about 70 dreams and even more visions. In both the Old Testament and the New Testament they are considered as revelations coming from God. "Those who un-derstood the revelations God has given them, such as Abra-ham and Solomon, became great and wise; those who were overcome by their inner experience, such as Paul or Ezekiel, became great missionaries and prophets". (Sanford, 1989, 94). Other people were chosen by God to interpret dreams like Joseph or Daniel, and they were highly honoured by all.

- Dreams in the Bible are God's breakthrough into human his-tory, God's breakthrough into the human consciousness via the unconscious.

- Dreams and visions in the Bible are considered to be similar and show a profound religious experience.

- The early Church regarded dreams the same way as in the OT being revelations from God.

Today, people generally do not like to depend on dreams or visions in order to contemplate God. Many want to find God through rational thinking. They want creeds and dogmas and not religious interior ex-periences or inspiration. And indeed "it is a fearful thing to fall into the hands of the living God", as the letter to the Hebrews tells us (10:31).

But if we consider that dreams come from our soul (unconscious) which always wants to help us, then I think we should allow God's disturbing presence to come to us in nightly dreams today.

Bibliography

Bandawe, Chiwoza. (2010). *Practical uMunthu Psychology*, Balaka: Montfort Media.

Bauer, Johannes B. (1981). *Encyclopedia of Biblical Theology*. New York: Crossroad.

Drewermann, Eugen. (1987). *Tiefenpsychologie und Exegese, Band 1, Traum, Mythos, Märchen, Sage und Legende*. Olten: Walter Verlag

Sanford, John A. (1989). *Dreams, God's forgotten Language*. San Francisco: Harper and Row.

Slater, George A. (1995). *Bringing Dreams to Life, Learning to interpret your dreams.* New York: Paulist Press

2

The dream of Jacob, Gen. 28: 10 – 22

Gotthard Rosner

As we have seen in the first article, dreams in the Bible are very frequent, especially in the books of Genesis, Daniel and Ezekiel. They are considered to be revelations coming from God and help to continue salvation history. In Gen 28 we find the dream of Jacob. According to psychology we here could speak of a "pre-cognitive dream", or a "deja-vu" dream which signifies a dream that is influenced by the recent past of a person.

The Setting or Context

In Gen. 27 Jacob cheats his brother Esau and steals his father's blessing through fraud. Esau was the first born and according to the Israelite culture should have received Isaac's blessing first. By cheating and pretending to be Esau, Jacob received the blessing and the promise of a great future.

Only afterwards does Jacob understand the consequences of his action. In order to save his life, he has to run away. He faces a life of a fugitive in a strange country (Haran), among strange people.

The contents of the dream

At night, full of fear and insecurity Jacob dreams. He sees a ladder (better staircase) being extended between heaven and earth. Angels are coming down and going up. God himself comes down and stands besides Jacob. He renews the promises made to Abraham and Isaac, to the ancestors of Israel. Jacob will become a great nation and will inherit the land that he now has to leave.

The symbols of the dream:

There are two:

- The ladder or staircase: It signifies a bridge between heaven and earth, between God and human kind. It also signifies the up and down of human life. It is a universal or archetypal symbol, understood and used all over the world. If we think of a ladder or staircase, we think normally of going up and less of coming down. One may think of the African story of the rope, which connected God and humanity – which came to be cut by people because of jealousy.

- The angels ascending and descending: The angels are messengers from God. Here they are a symbol of communion with God. Human beings participate in the divine world. The symbol wants to encourage Jacob to continue his journey and gives him new strength and energy.

The meaning of the dream

Although Jacob has to run away to save his life, God still continues his covenant with him as he did with Abraham. Jacob will return, inherit the land and become a great nation. The dream encourages him not to be afraid and not to give up. A new responsibility is given to him: He is the heir of God's promises. The promise, however, is not for Jacob alone, but also for his descendants, the twelve tribes of Israel. There is a social dimension to this dream.

Did Jacob understand the dream?

I think he did. He called the place where he had been sleeping "the gate to heaven" and the "house of God". This explains the name of the sanctuary found there which is Bethel = the house of El (God). It also explains the fact that the ancestors of Israel paid a tithe to this sanctuary every year. Through the dream Jacob realised that God was with him and that he had become the heir of the promise. The dream reveals God's plan not only to Jacob, but also to us, because the real bridge between God and humanity will be Jesus Christ. He is the true gate to heaven. John 1:51 applies the dream of Jacob to Jesus Christ: "You will see the heavens opened and the angels of God ascending and descending upon the Son of Man".

GOTTHARD ROSNER

3

Dreams in the Catholic Church: lessons from Church history

Bernhard Udelhoven

> *... I will pour out my Spirit on everyone. Your sons and your daughters will prophesy, your young men will see visions, and your old men will dream dreams.* (Acts 2:17)

> *... They say, 'I had a dream! I had a dream!' How long will this continue in the hearts of these lying prophets, who prophesy the delusions of their own minds?* (Jeremiah 23:25-26.)

In the Bible, God spoke to his chosen ones in dreams; the same Bible also shares experiences of dream delusions, and warns about the search for guidance through dreams.

With such a mixed Biblical heritage, how did the Church deal with divine dreams in its long history? Which rules and principles of discernment did the Church develop?

Dreams in the early persecuted Church

In the early Church it was taken for granted that God reveals his will through dreams and that dreams can give access to the presence of God. Pagans in the Roman Empire converted to Christianity on account of their dreams. In times of persecution of Christians it was even expected from God to speak to his saints through dreams, especially to those chosen or destined to be martyrs.[1]

Divine dreams were relevant to the Church and gave to the Church symbols and images of heavenly realities that cannot be seen with

---

[1] See Lien-Yueh Wei (2011).

the human eye. By sharing the dreams of the saints, believers gained access to a mystic spirituality where heaven was near and open, God alive and very personal. God could communicate with his saints through dreams, since dreams were one of the languages that God spoke (Tertullian). Meeting with God in dreams, however, presented the dreamer also with an all-demanding call that implied a readiness to give one's life in martyrdom.

A revealing example can be found in the dreams of Perpetua, an African saint. Perpetua kept a diary with a dream journal during her last days in prison while awaiting execution. After her death this diary was published together with an account of her martyrdom by an anonymous writer. The account was widely read; a number of theologians (including Tertullian and Augustine) used her dreams for their different arguments. Historians regard the prison diary to be authentic. Also from the aspect of modern psychology the dream narratives are regarded as genuine.[2]

Perpetua was a married woman, 22 years old, nursing a baby, and still a catechumen, when she was arrested in Carthage by the Roman authorities on account of her conversion to Christianity. In her group was also Felicitas, a pregnant slave, who was to give birth to her baby two days before their execution. The deacon Saturus, who had been instructing them, was absent at the time of their arrest; he handed himself in to the authorities voluntarily so as to be martyred together with his group. While in prison, Perpetua wrote down the context of her dream experiences:

> After a few days we were taken into the dungeon, and I was very much afraid, because I had never felt such darkness. ... I was very unusually distressed by my anxiety for my infant. ... I suckled my child, which was now enfeebled with hunger. In my anxiety for it, I addressed my mother and comforted my brother, and commended to their care my son. I was languishing because I had seen them languishing on my account. Such solicitude I suffered for many days, and I obtained for my infant to remain in the dungeon with me; and forthwith I grew strong and was relieved from

---

[2] See Farina (2009), 4ff; Davies (2005).

distress and anxiety about my infant; and the dungeon became to me as it were a palace, so that I preferred being there to being elsewhere. Then my brother said to me, 'My dear sister, you are already in a position of great dignity, and are such that you may ask for a vision, and that it may be made known to you whether this is to result in a passion or an escape.' And I, who knew that I was privileged to converse with the Lord, whose kindnesses I had found to be so great, boldly promised him, and said, 'Tomorrow I will tell you.' And I asked, and this was what was shown me [in a dream]:

The first dream of Perpetua

I saw a golden ladder of marvellous height, reaching up even to heaven, and very narrow, so that persons could only ascend it one by one; and on the sides of the ladder was fixed every kind of iron weapon. There were swords, lances, hooks, daggers; so that if any one went up carelessly, or not looking upwards, he would be torn to pieces and his flesh would cleave to the iron weapons. And under the ladder itself was crouching a dragon of wonderful size, who lay in wait for those who ascended, and frightened them from the ascent. And Saturus went up first, who had subsequently delivered himself up freely on our account, not having been present at the time that we were taken prisoners. And he attained the top of the ladder, and turned towards me, and said to me, 'Perpetua, I am waiting for you; but be careful that the dragon does not bite you.' And I said, 'In the name of the Lord Jesus Christ, he shall not hurt me.' And from under the ladder itself, as if in fear of me, he slowly lifted up his head; and as I trod upon the first step, I trod upon his head.

And I went up, and I saw an immense extent of garden, and in the midst of the garden a white-haired man sitting in the dress of a shepherd, of a large stature, milking sheep; and standing around were many thousand white-robed ones. And he raised his head, and looked upon me, and said to me, 'You are welcome, daughter.' And he called me, and from the cheese as he was milking he gave me as it were a little cake, and I received it with folded hands; and I ate it, and all who stood around said Amen. And at the sound of their voices I was awakened, still tasting a sweetness which I cannot describe. And I immediately related this to my brother, and we understood that it was to be a passion, and we ceased henceforth to have any hope in this world.[3]

The dream is loaded with Biblical and Christian symbols: the ladder going up to heaven, the dragon, her stepping on the head of the beast, the shepherd, the liturgical greeting ('Amen') after she receives the heavenly food (cheese). (Note that cheese in the time of Perpetua was eaten during the Agape-meals.)[4]

Perpetua saw in the difficult ladder going up to heaven, spiked with dangerous weapons of torture, a sign of her upcoming martyrdom. Martyrdom was also foreshadowed in the symbol of milk that had turned into solid cheese: among Christians in Perpetua's time, milk was regarded symbolically as food for infants, signifying Christians who were still immature; solids (milk turned into cheese) were seen symbolically as foods for adults, those ready for martyrdom.[5] In the eyes of the Church and maybe also in her own eyes, Perpetua was still an "infant", a catechumen, still to grow strong in the Christian faith, yet the dream showed that she was to become an "adult" through her early martyrdom. After the dream, Perpetua stopped reflecting about possible escapes, but saw that the will of God was leading her to her forthcoming death.

The dream symbols thus were given theological meanings by the early Church. At the same time, they also portrayed very personal meanings fully bound up with the unique life-experience of Perpetua. The day before the dream, her family was still pleading with her to renounce her faith for the sake of the baby not yet weaned, which left Perpetua with a very difficult choice to make – between the duty towards her baby and family, and her desire not to denounce her faith.

---

[3] *The Martyrdom of Perpetua and Felicity* (translated by Rev, R. E. Wallis), chapter 1:3

[4] Agape meals were described by Tertullian, her contemporary citizen of Carthage, and also by Hippolytus. See Lien-Yueh Wei (2011), 212.

[5] Building on 1 Cor 3:2, Hippolytus of Rome and Clement of Alexandria, living in the time of Perpetua, referred to cheese as the solid food of milk, while Origen linked solid food to martyrdom. (Davis (2005))

The dream encouraged Perpetua to make a leap of faith: to keep her eyes fixed on heaven always "looking upwards" on the journey up the ladder, all alone, "less one would be torn into pieces" along the way (torn into pieces by weapons of martyrdom, but also by her worries for family and baby). A modern psychologist suggested that the dream symbol of milk from a milking shepherd turning into cheese was interwoven with her own embodied experience of disrupted breastfeeding and worries about the future of her baby after her execution.[6] After receiving and consuming the cheese, she woke up still feeling the sweet taste in her mouth; she gave up "hope in this world" for the "sweetness which I cannot describe" found in heaven. Baby and family she left in the care of God.

Divine dreams were seen by the early Church as occasions where a person actually tasted heaven and experienced the fulfilment of God's promise while still on earth. They were seen as a sheer act of grace authored by God. At the same time also divine dreams were building their symbolic worlds on the dreamers' own embodied experiences. Synesius of Cyrene (whose teaching on dreams was very influential in early Christian times) encouraged people to seek guidance on their way to God through dreams, and even dream divinations. At the same time he ridiculed the use of dream manuals or lists of common dream symbols as if one could look at a dream other than in relation to the dreamer's own life-history and experience.[7] Divine dreams come from God; at the same time the dream language is intimately related to the life-history and life-experience of the dreamer who dreams the dream. A dream cannot be interpreted in the abstract, but must be read side by side with life-story of the dreamer. Many hundred years later, St. Thomas Aquinas expressed this in the principle that *"grace builds on nature"*: grace does not negate the natural world and its principle, but works right through the natural world, sanctifying it from within. The whole natural world was for St. Thomas a "theatre" or a "stage" of grace. Also divine dreams pass right through the human faculties, including the person's own symbolic world attained by his/her life-experience. Today one would say

---

[6] Davis (2005).
[7] Synesius of Cyrene, *On Dreams*. Note however that Synesius wrote this text (encouraging divination through dreams) before his conversion to Christianity.

that divine dreams are co-authored by God and by the human unconscious activities of the mind.

The last dream of St. Perpetua (the night before her martyrdom)

I saw in a vision that Pomponius the deacon came hither to the gate of the prison, and knocked vehemently. I went out to him, and opened the gate for him; and he was clothed in a richly ornamented white robe... And he said to me, 'Perpetua, we are waiting for you; come!' And he held his hand to me, and we began to go through rough and winding places. Scarcely at length had we arrived breathless at the amphitheatre, when he led me into the middle of the arena, and said to me, 'Do not fear, I am here with you, and I am labouring with you;' and he departed. And I gazed upon an immense assembly in astonishment. And because I knew that I was given to the wild beasts, I marvelled that the wild beasts were not let loose upon me. Then there came forth against me a certain Egyptian, horrible in appearance, with his backers, to fight with me. And there came to me, as my helpers and encouragers, handsome youths; and I was stripped, and became a man. Then my helpers began to rub me with oil, as is the custom for contest; and I beheld that Egyptian on the other hand rolling in the dust.

And a certain man came forth, of wondrous height, so that he even over-topped the top of the amphitheatre; and he wore a loose tunic and a purple robe ..., as if he were a trainer of gladiators, and a green branch upon which were apples of gold. And he called for silence, and said, 'This Egyptian, if he should overcome this woman, shall kill her with the sword; and if she shall conquer him, she shall receive this branch.' Then he departed. And we drew near to one another, and began to deal out blows. He sought to lay hold of my feet, while I struck at his face with my heels; and I was lifted up in the air, and began thus to thrust at him as if spurning the earth. But when I saw that there was some delay I joined my hands so as to twine my fingers with one another; and I took hold upon his head, and he fell on his face, and I trod upon his head. And the people began to shout, and my backers to exult. And I drew near to the trainer and took the branch; and he kissed me, and said to me, 'Daughter, peace be with you,' and I began to go gloriously to the Sanavivarian gate. Then I awoke, and perceived that I was not to fight with beasts, but against the devil. Still I knew that the victory was awaiting me.[8]

The dream again is full of faith-symbols: the horrible Egyptian rolling in dust (understood by Perpetua as a symbol for the Devil); the oil with which she is anointed for the fight (one may think of the oil of catechumens in the fight against the Devil); stepping on the head of the Egyptian (one may think again of the head of the serpent crashed by the new Eve); the figure of the glorious trainer of gladiators (one may think of Christ as the trainer or maker of martyrs); the branch of life with golden apples that the judge-figure holds (understood by her as the wreath of life with its fruits of immortality); his liturgical greeting ("peace be with you"). The following day Perpetua was going to be mauled by a wild cow and then killed by the sword in the arena of Carthage. The crowd of the stadium was to cheer at Perpetua's death, while the dream shows the heavenly saints applauding for Perpetua. Dreams in early Christianity showed to believers the underlying meaning of events through the eyes of the heavenly realities.

In her dream, Perpetua discovers that she has turned into a man, ready to fight. The early Church looked at this as the grace of spiritual transformation. Having turned into a man, Perpetua was becoming herself a Christ-figure through her martyrdom, no longer restrained by the weaknesses of her own natural body in the fight against the Devil.[9]

While thus looking at the dream symbols in a theological manner, one should never lose sight of Perpetua's inner life that gave rise to the dream. Perpetua herself was very careful to record her own worries and deep feelings that anticipated the dream. The dream symbol of "becoming a man" reflects also her own struggles with her family, shedding light upon her own changing relationship with her father.

---

[8] *The Martyrdom of Perpetua and Felicity* (translated by Rev, R. E. Wallis), chapter 3:2
[9] See Frieman (n.d.)

She loved her father and had always respected his authority. When her father came repeatedly to prison, often with her baby in arms, first in full awareness of his authority as father and head of the family: ordering and demanding, later by humiliating himself, begging and pleading on his knees and in tears, to renounce her faith for the sake of the family, she had opted for disobedience; she wrote in her diary about the pain which this caused to her. Her father started to call her no longer his daughter; he referred to her as "domina" (as did her brother before) – a term which may refer to a lady (no longer related), but also to a female head of a household. Perpetua's relationship to her father was no longer one of cultural subordination; she had become the stronger partner in the relationship. After being stripped naked in the dream, she discovered that she had turned into a man ready to fight. Indeed, in many cultural aspects she was no longer a woman: by going against her duties in regards to her father and her husband, by taking the legal advocacy into her own hands in her encounter with the judge (who pleaded with Perpetua to listen to her father), and by going to become a public figure in the arena, the sphere of men. During her martyrdom Perpetua became the spokesperson for all the martyrs dying with her, including the men.

Instead of the father, it is the Christ-figure or God-figure who calls her "my daughter" in the dream. Spiritual transformation (becoming a daughter of God) had social and political consequences: it changed her relationships to her family, her culture, and her society.

Early theology of dreams

In the first centuries of the Church, the Church Fathers laid the foundation for Christian dream theories. Apart from recording the divine dreams of ancient martyrs (for example dreams of the saints Polycarp, Perpetua, Agatha, Lucy, and Catherine of Alexandria), many of the Church Fathers had themselves experienced divine dreams that shaped their lives and faith (Cyprian of Carthage, Gregory of Nyssa, Jerome, Ambrose, Martin of Tours). When St. Irenaeus expounded on the Biblical dreams and visions of the prophets and apostles, he noted that God cannot be seen with the human eye, while images ("similitudes") of his glory, as well as events of the future, can be conveyed to the soul in dreams and visions.[10]

Yet it was also very clear to the early Church that not all dreams that seem to come from God, do come from God. The Church Fathers distanced themselves strongly from the Gnostics, who looked towards dreams and visions as direct infusions of divine and superior knowledge, which brought them into conflict with Church authority and doctrine. Later also Montanus and his followers (including Tertullian) broke away from the Church on account of Montanus' dreams and visions during outbursts of fits. Reliance on dreams brought schisms and divisions; many desert monks started to warn about spiritual delusions, which could even be obtained in idealistic ascetic efforts. St. Irenaeus refuted erring doctrines to which Valentinus had arrived through a series of dreams concerning divine beings and offspring. The method which Irenaeus applied became a "triple yardstick" for dealing with dreams: he compared the dream symbols and conclusions first with Scripture, then with the Creed, then finally with the consensus of the Church.[11]

Another means of discernment of dreams for the early Church was to look at the inner movements of the soul that the dream stirs up. From the nature of the movements one can discern the origin of the dream: God's dreams bring inner peace and courage; dreams of demons bring distracted excitement. St. Ambrose (endorsing the advice of St. Anthony) explained this with these words:

> When, therefore, they [demons] come by night to you and wish to tell the future, or say 'We are the angels,' give no heed, for they lie. . . . But if they shamelessly stand their ground, capering, and change their forms of appearance, fear them not, nor shrink, nor heed them as though they were good spirits. For the presence either of the good or evil by the help of God can easily be distinguished. The vision of the holy ones is not fraught with distraction: 'For they will not strive, nor cry, nor shall anyone hear their voice' [Matt 12:19; cf. Is. 42:2]. But it comes quietly and

---

[10] Irenaeus, *Against Heresies,* Book 4, 20:11.

[11] Irenaeus, *Against Heresies,* Book 1.

gently that an immediate joy, gladness, and courage arise in the soul. For the Lord who is our joy is with them, and the power of God the Father.[12]

This method of looking at the inner movements of the heart goes back to the discernment of spirits as proposed by St. Paul himself: "Do not quench the Spirit. Do not despise prophetic utterances. Test everything; retain what is good" (1 Thess. 5:19–21). Paul's way of testing the spirits was to look at the fruits: the fruits of the spirit (charity, joy, peace, endurance, kindness, goodness, faithfulness, gentleness, self-control) can be discerned easily from the fruits of the flesh (sexual immorality, jealousy, witchcraft, discord, jealousy, fits of rage, envy, etc.) Many centuries later St. Ignatius of Loyola was to adapt and elaborate these rules of discernment to prayer and meditations, by reflecting on his own experiences when looking at the movements of his heart.

Also after the difficult controversies with the Gnostics and with Montanus on accounts of dreams, Christians continued to be confronted with popular pagan dream divination systems. The Church condemned strongly the manipulation of dreams and the practice of divination through them. Divine dreams were a gift of grace, and could not be obtained through methods or techniques. Cyril of Jerusalem and Gregory of Nyssa denounced the treatment of dreams as omens.[13] The first Council of Ankara (314) condemned the search for dream revelations, and warnings were issued against dream interpretation as a pagan form of divination.

When a person heard the voice of God in a dream, it could have many possible origins, and even multiple origins. For the early Church, dreams were seen to originate mainly in the human psyche and the soul; some of the Fathers (for example Tertullian) speculated also on the influence of the human body, diet, times and seasons. Dreams could give indications for the state of body and mind, but more specifically of the soul; they were regarded as a window into the soul, a tool for self-knowledge. At the same time the soul, itself spiritual, was seen to be open to the spiritual world: Dreams could

---

[12] Ambrose, *Life of St. Anthony*, chapter 35.
[13] See Lehrer (2008).

come from God and angels, but they could also come from the Devil, demons, and black magic.[14] Also saints could appear in dreams. (According to ancient traditions, St. Ignatius of Antioch appeared to his disciples after his martyrdom, and St. Agatha appeared to Lucy). However, with the exception to the saints, dreams could not come from the dead. When Augustine was asked about dreams of the dead, he replied: dreaming of a dead person does not imply that this person has appeared, as little as one would expect a living person to know that one has dreamt of him.[15]

The Church's Christian reflections on dreams developed often in a marked distinction from their contemporary cultural background. The writings of Tertullian on dreams, which became very influential in the Church, developed in a political climate where an unfavourable dream of the emperor (and other high standing officials) could bring a person to prison and execution, as could the dream of a person about the emperor. Tertullian saw in this an abuse of dreams: the prime locus of a dream was the inner world of a person, not the political arena. Tertullian developed his theology of dreams also against the popular philosophical background of the Stoics, a philosophical school, where a person was expected, through self-discipline and willpower, to control even one's own dreams. According to Stoic teachings, a good person dreams noble acts, while a bad person dreams bad ones. Tertullian set a sharp contrast to this teaching when he said that "good acts committed during a dream are without merit and bad acts without blame".[16]

The Church evaluated sin with an emphasis on intention, free will and reason; it became a Christian maxim that "you cannot sin while you sleep", when all these faculties seem suspended. Similar to Tertullian, also John Chrysostom explained that "to do or say anything dis-

---

[14] Examples: Ignatius of Antioch, *Letter to the Philippians, chapter* 4; Justin the Martyr, *The First Apology of Justin*, chapter 14; Clement of Alexandria, *Paedagogus*, book 5, Chapter 9; Irenaeus, *Against Heresies*, Book 1, Chapter 13; Senesius of Cyrene, *Concerning Dreams*;Tertullian, *A Treatise on the Soul*, chapters 45-49; Augustine, *Anti-Pelagian Writings*.

[15] Augustine, *On Care to be had for the Dead*, chapter 12. He guessed that such visions were due to angelic operations on the psyche which made the dead appear to be doing or saying something to the dreamer. Note however that a number of Church Fathers acknowledged the apparition of saints, especially martyrs, after their death. See Lien-Yueh Wei (2011), 56, footnote 72.

[16] See Weidhorn (1965), 76.

graceful in a dream is of no consequence; the disgrace is lost with the sleep and is not punishable".[17] One was not accountable for committing murder, theft, rape, or incest in a dream; neither would dream action ontologically affect the Christian 'self'. While it is true that dreams can mirror moral faults or lead a person to commit moral faults (after waking up), the dreams in themselves are "absolved" in the teaching of the early Church from any sin and virtue.

This Christian outlook placed dreams on a more reflective level, but did not take away their essential value, both as a tool for self-knowledge and for communicating with God. Dreams were recognised as a sacred space, where God could intervene with his own language.

Dreams in the Christian Middle Ages

The heritage of the Church Fathers on dreams coincided partly with a worldview marked by the philosophy of Neo-Platonism: the spiritual world was seen as determining the physical world; the unseen spiritual dimensions were given priority over the events which met the physical eye. Dreams were seen as a window into the spiritual world. Spiritual dreams and visions could help an erring person to come back on track towards a perfect and happy life. The outlook on the world in Neo-Platonism was positive and benevolent: evil was not seen to exist in itself; evil was but the absence of good.

After Augustine (and the collapse of the Roman Empire), the Church's outlook on the world became much more pessimistic: human nature was mainly seen in its intrinsic sinfulness. This meant that also human dreams remained trapped in this sinful condition.

For many Desert Fathers, an awareness of one's own sinfulness was a greater grace than a heavenly dream or vision. "How is it that some can say, 'We see visions of angels?' Happier by far is he who can see his own sins at all times." [18]

---

[17] Ibid.
[18] See McNierney (n.d.)

Ideals of holiness were portrayed as heroic efforts (and often very lonely efforts) to conquer and overcome human weakness through ascetic repentance. Divine dreams became the privilege of very few extraordinary saints and spiritual supermen. Ordinary people were no longer seen as having access to the heavenly world through dreams – not even priests, monks or nuns. This made dreams of ordinary Christians pretty useless, if not dangerous.

Also Scholastic theology tended to devalue dreams, but for different reasons. Scholastic theology had a positive view of creation, seen as basically good; the human mind, assisted by God's grace, was judged as being capable of reaching God through a contemplation of creation (Rom 1:20) and natural law. On this upwards journey to God, primacy was given to truths obtained by the intelligent mind through logical conclusions and abstract scrutiny. Dreams here could play only a very secondary role. Also the possibility of a connection between dreams and demons instilled fear; messages in dreams were easily grouped together with the phenomena of clairvoyance, premonition, and telepathy. Though such gifts were also associated with the ancient saints, they easily attained a connotation of black magic and the demonic; they became gifts to be dismissed, not to be used. Also an emphasis on the authority of the Church did not encourage an attending to dreams. Christian spirituality came to be identified with official dogmas and practices accessed through the use of reason. Dreams were called phantasms; they could still strengthen a person's faith, but were largely pushed into the private sphere.

Note however that St. Thomas Aquinas, the master of Scholastic theology, was silenced by three consecutive divine dreams; the dreams put an end to his writing, and made him consider his own extensive work, the "Summa", to be nothing but straw. It should also be noted that parallel to Scholastic thought, important traditions of monastic theology developed, which gave much more room for dreams. A sensual spirituality matured in monasteries where divine love was depicted with erotic images. The images of the Song of Songs in the Bible were rediscovered and applied to mystical spirituality; sensual images could become a ladder for climbing towards God. In such a theology, dreams could play a very different role. Many mystics of this monastic tradition crafted their Christian 'self' in reference to their dreams.[19] While this spirituality never disappeared, it was certainly side-lined by Scholasticism in late-medieval university based theology.

Dreams in the Modern Era

After the Reformation and the religious wars in Europe, the Catholic Church was no longer in the driving seat for determining the truth about the nature of dreams. Enlightenment thinking with its pervasive mood of freethinking and radical questioning, experimentation and discovery through rational enquiry, brought a new human self-understanding which accompanied the American and French revolutions (freedom, equality, brotherhood), and spread through Europe. Enlightened people were supposed to be tolerant towards different religious traditions, but no longer willing to submit under Church dogmas without own critical engagement. Dreams did not flourish in an enlightened culture which stressed universal laws, not individual and private dream revelations, which could not be verified or objectified. Constant scientific revolutions and world-changing progress somehow proved to the enlightened world the primacy of rational universal thought with an unbounded optimism about the future. Dreams were marginalised into the realm of the irrational; irrational thought, like superstition, was something to be overcome and defeated, since it blocked progress. Dreams belonged to the realm of personal opinions, but public life should be governed by self-evident universal thought.

The Enlightenment developed its own cultural counterpart: the Romantic Movement. While many people in the wake of the Enlightenment felt disenchanted with the world, with nature, in a climate of dominant emphasis on rational thought, the Romantics stressed the unique individual, originality, and individual creativity through arts and music. To understand the world, one first needs to understand oneself. The Romantics valued introspection over objective external observation. This gave dreams a new value: dreams became again a tool for self-knowledge. An awareness of the uniqueness of the inner self in turn gave the Romantics a sense of mission to change the

---

[19] Lehrer (2008).

world. A personal unique dream could give the person a mission for the whole world.[20] (This was also witnessed within the Church: personal dreams of Don Bosco, of Daniel Comboni or of Charles Lavigerie, gave them a sense of vocation for the world.)

With the beginning of the 20th century, Sigmund Freud somehow tried to bridge the gap between the two different outlooks on dreams. Freud gave the Romantics a tool for self-understanding and introspection, by seeing in dreams the "royal road to the unconscious" and by basing his method on the free associations that the dreamer made out of his/her own dream symbols. At the same time he proposed that dreams follow strictly a universal logic of their own, which can be investigated with the help of a few basic concepts and principles. Here he stood fully in the tradition of the Enlightenment.

The Church at large remained hostile towards the universal grand theories about human nature that Enlightenment thinkers proposed, often no longer with reference to God. At the same time many aspects of the new worldviews became compelling also for the Church and for theology. In regards to dreams, the Church took many insights from modern psychology, which brought dreams back onto its own agenda, without, however, dissolving Christian spirituality into psychology. Christian spirituality maintained its essential orientation towards God, who is immanent but also transcendent.

As a tool for approaching divine dreams, the Catholic Church developed the concepts of public and private revelation:

> *Throughout the ages, there have been so-called 'private' revelations, some of which have been recognized by the authority of the Church. They do not belong, however, to the deposit of faith. It is not their role to improve or complete Christ's definitive revelation, but to help live more fully by it in a certain period of history. Guided by the magisterium of the Church, the sensus fidelium [the collective sense of the faithful] knows how to discern and welcome in these revelations whatever constitutes an authentic call of Christ or his saints to the Church. Christian faith cannot accept 'revelations' that claim to surpass or correct the revelation of*

---

[20] See Henry (1998).

which Christ is the fulfilment, as is the case in certain non-Christian religions and also in certain recent sects which base themselves on such 'revelations'" (Catechism of the Catholic Church, 67. See also Dei Verbum 4 of Vatican II)

Conclusion

This small exposition shows that attitudes and expectations towards divine dreams changed throughout the history of the Church and were also somehow linked to a particular worldview of what human nature is about. Attitudes about dreams, however, did not prevent any dream to be dreamt, in season and out of season. The early Church regarded dreams as a "sacred space" (Lien-Yueh Wei) where God can meet any person, rich and poor alike, the saint as well as the sinner. Maybe modern psychology has helped the Church to go back to this openness and help people to prepare this sacred space, honour it, and listen to it.

Bibliography

1.   Patristic Church Fathers.

The following materials were accessed through this link:

http://patristics.org/resources/early-christian-texts/

> Ambrose: *Life of St. Anthony*;
> Augustine: *On Care to be had for the Dead*;
> Augustine: *Anti-Pelagian Writings*;
> Clement of Alexandria: *Paedagogus*;
> Ignatius of Antioch: *Letter to the Phillipians*;
> Irenaeus of Lyon: *Against Heresies*;
> Justin the Martyr: *The First Apology of Justin*;
> Senesius of Cyrene: *Concerning Dreams*;
> Tertullian: *A Treatise on the Soul*.

2. Academic sources:

Davis, P. M. (2005). The weaning of Perpetua: Female embodiment and spiritual growth metaphor in the dream of an early Christian martyr. In *Dreaming* 2005, December, pp. 261-270.

Farina, W. (2009). *Perpetua of Carthage: Portrait of a Third-Century Martyr.* North Carolina: McFarland.

Frieman, R. (n.d.). *Ancient Carthage.* Retrieved May 19, 2012, from http://ancientcarthage.wikispaces.com/Passio+Perpetuae+et+Felicitatis

Henry, M. D. (1998). The Enlightenment and Romanticism from a Theological Perspective. In *International Theological Quarterly, 63* (3), pp. 250-262.

Lehrer, P. (2008). *The Journey Inward: Crafting the Christian Self through Autobiography, Dreams and Vision.* (PhD Philosophy, Graduate School of Theology. Retrieved August 31, 2011, from http://www.gtfeducation.org/academics/OTL/OTL_Lehrer.pdf

Lien-Yueh Wei, S. (2011). *Doctrinalising Dreams: Patristic Views of the Nature of Dreams and their Relation to Early Christian Doctrines.* PhD, University of Edinburgh.

Lien-Yueh Wei, S. (n.d). *The Nature of Perpetua's Dreams: The Theological Meanings and Significance of Sacred Dreams.* Retrieved May 19, 2012, from http://christ.org.tw/dream/dreams/nature_of_perpetua_dreams.htm

MacNierney, M. (n.d.) *The Dark Speech of God: Dreams and Visions in Ancient Christianity.* Retrieved May 19, 2012, from http://www.uky.edu/~aubel2/eng104/dreams/pdf/mcnierney.pdf

Wallis, R. E. (n.d.) *Perpetua the Martyr.* Retrieved on May 19, 2012, from http://www.amyrachelpeterson.com/Groups/1000004968/S

aint_Perpetua/Perpetua_The_Martyr/Read_Perpetuas_Priso
n/Read_Perpetuas_Prison.aspx

Weidhorn, M. (1965). Dreams and Guilt. *Harward Theological Review,
58* (1), 69-90.

4

Zambian traditions concerning dreams

Bernhard Udelhoven

In this paper I look at some aspects of Zambian traditions towards dreams. It is based on seminars conducted with the "Fingers of Thomas" (a research group working with FENZA) in a variety of Parishes, with Prayer Guides (Archdiocese of Lusaka), and on interviews with persons (pastors, elders, and traditional healers) known for their contributions to dream interpretation.[1] We cannot provide a systematic theory on Zambian understandings of dreams, but intend to give a voice to dream experiences across different Zambian cultures that can give some insights not only into popular dream notions but also into fundamental questions about human nature.

While a number of people devalued dreams (sometimes in response to Church teaching), most people took it for granted that dreams constitute a valuable and necessary source of information: We were told that dreams announce deaths in the family. Dreams announce future events that are to come (fortunes, misfortunes or sickness). Dreams warn the dreamer about the activities of harmful people and spirits that are around. Dreams can manifest the harmful activities of witches and Satanists. No doubt, dreams are tied to a deep-seated understanding about the nature of human life and the human person.

---

[1] Traditional healers: Dr Sitali (Bauleni), Dr Ngoi (Bauleni), Dr Tembo (Kanyama), Dr Eliyah (Woodlands), Dr Malama Chishimba (Bauleni), Dr Maria (Bauleni). Elders: Mr Bernard Mubanga (Kabwata), Mr Francis Mupinde (Kabwata), Mr & Mrs JJ Mulenga (Bauleni), Mrs Phiri (St. Ignatius), Mrs Daka (Bauleni), Mr & Mrs Zulu (Chilenje-South), Mr & Mrs Banda (Bauleni), Mrs Mumba (Woodlands), Mr & Mrs Chansa (Woodlands), Chisasa Mucengwa (Yongolo), Mweni John (Yongolo). Pastors: Bishop Mcheka (Bauleni, Jesus Ministries), Pastor Salome Phiri (Bauleni, New Revelation Bible Church), Pastor Memory Simutanda (Bauleni, Christ Believers), Bishop Katobemo (Bauleni, Glorious Salvation Ministries), Pastor Phiri Mvula (Bauleni, Triumphant Entry), Pastor Josephe (Bauleni, Paradise Spirit Church). For more information on the "Fingers of Thomas", see http://fenza.org/fingers-of-thomas.html.

Dreams also are seen as an important medium through which God (or the ancestors) can speak. Dream images attributed to God can be strikingly stereotyped. Bengt Sundkler, in his studies of dreams in South African Churches, reports on such standardised dream narratives and symbols across the board of Churches: from prophetic Zion-type up to the mainstream mission Churches.[2] Such symbols in divine dreams are also common in Zambia. Pastors, prayer leaders and healers narrated to us dream experiences in which they met Jesus, or an angel, or a person with a shining face. One man dreamt of crossing an enormously high bridge over water into another realm of life, after which he was being anointed to cure. He has become a prominent person in the healing ministry in Lusaka.[3] Some people had changed their religious life-orientation in response to dreams. One nurse had left the Catholic Church in response to a dream in which she saw the founder of the Mutima Church (Emilio Mulolani), which she subsequently joined.

Dreams from heaven come in readily comprehensible symbols, but so do dreams from hostile and evil spiritual forces. In our studies on Satanism in Zambia we documented a variety of standardised and stereotyped dream symbols and visions – shared by different dreamers across different provinces – of the underworld, featuring the ocean and waterfalls, blood and sacrifices, people wearing black clothes, snakes and monsters, queens and princes, venues of "Nigeria" and "USA" as well as certain suspected Churches.[4]

Also many traditional healers (*ng'anga*) experienced their calling in dreams. Two healers spoke to us about the medicines they use so as to enhance dream experiences and acquire the gift of seeing things in dreams. The medicines used may give a glimpse into the symbolic or spiritual universes to which dreams can be linked: One healer was given incisions with medicines made of the roots of the *Kangwa* tree (*Ziziphus abyssinica*)[5] taken from a graveyard, pounded together with soil and ashes taken from the left-overs of a funeral fire, the brains of a hyena (known for its night activities), the brains of the *nkubi* bird (a

---

[2] Sundkler (1961), 265ff.

[3] We have documented some experiences in previous publications: Mumbi (2010); Udelhoven (2010, 2011).

[4] Udelhoven (2009).

[5] All botanic names in this essay are taken from Storrs (1995).

vulture known for its ability and intelligence to find a dead body many miles away), and the brain of the *cikwekwe* bird (of the species of roller, which is said to announce funerals back in the village when one bird is found leaving its companions in a falling flight). These medicines were seen to link up the healer spiritually to dream-knowledge that comes from the realm of the dead, the realm of animals that are mystically connected with human affairs, the night, the dark and the hidden, across large distances. Also another healer used the Kangwa tree for dreams: taking two of its leaves, opposing them, piercing and pinning them together with a straw taken from the roof of a funeral house, which he said he places under his pillow to receive dreams of knowledge. The same doctor also said he collects, wherever he sees it, grass that grows on tree-stumps (*fishiki*, constituting hidden obstacles that cause people to stumble), which he adds into his bathing water, with the aim to induce dreams that reveal the hidden obstacles to his life or the lives of his clients.

Popular notions of dream interpretation

Since dreams are important for people, there exist side by side many different, sometimes contradictory, improvised systems of interpreting dream symbols. Many compelling dreams had a direct meaning for the people whom we interviewed; there was no need or little need for interpretation. "I dreamt of coffins, and the next day a close family member died". Other dreams, however, seemed more puzzling and indirect; as such they stood in need to be interpreted. A number of people knew of dream symbols with standardised meanings, which they were taught by family members or which they overheard elsewhere:

> To dream about rain (or a burning house) means death in the family. The rain is about tears flowing at the funeral.

> To dream about being given food to eat is a sign of witch-craft or initiation into Satanism.

> To dream about touching human faeces, or faeces of a dog, means death. (Some, however, said it means you become rich or find money.)

To dream about attacks by dogs or be encircled by fire are signs of witchcraft attacks.

To dream about catching a white fish is good luck. In the morning you should walk to the river. Black fish: somebody will die.

To dream about walking naked: be careful, somebody may be trying to bewitch you.

Quite a few people mentioned, however, that dreams can have the opposite of their apparent meaning:

When you dream of a wedding, it means you will have a funeral. When you dream of death it means birth. When you dream of picking up excreta, it means you will be rich.

Chaplin (1958) gave a list of dream symbol interpretations of a famous Nsenga headman known for dream analysis. What is interesting in the headman's list is that it does not only account for the dream symbols, but also for the "shape" of a dream and its proceedings and movements. Here some of his examples:

Dream: There is no change throughout the dream, either dancing or singing or something else pleasant all the time; but on waking you can remember little more than a general feeling of pleasure. Interpretation: This is a bad dream: for a man because his yet unborn child is likely to be stillborn or deformed, for a woman that a child will die.

Dream: A pleasant dream to begin with, often with music, but there is change and a friend will interrupt, but he goes away and the dream goes on as before. Interpretation: The man who comes into the dream may appear to be a friend, but really means to cheat you in some way.

Dream: You are travelling upwards towards heaven but at the top you see something unpleasant and drop down. You fail to reach the bottom and dream of something different. Interpretation: You are likely to have a serious sickness, but will eventually recover.

These were for the headman examples of indirect dreams. But there are also direct dreams, of which he himself was blessed, and also his grandson. Ancestors with powerful spirits could provoke an appearance:

> A typical 'direct-guidance' dream was this: 'A high shrill voice was heard and the dreamer told to stand up with his hands held palms upwards at face level, he was then directed to count slowly. At "four" the figure of his absent wife appeared standing in miniature on his hands, she stayed briefly then faded and the dream ended.' This was taken to indicate that she would arrive in four days' time; it should be recorded that she made a previously unexpected return at that time.

At the same time Chaplin also noted big differences in collections of dream symbols and their attributed meanings across Zambian tribes, and even across individuals within the same area.

Also today people are aware that there exist many different and often contradictory systems for interpreting dreams, sometimes within one's own family. Compare the following three statements which we collected:

- "To dream of a snake means there is witchcraft."

- "To dream of a snake means you have a demon."

- "To dream of a white snake means the blessings of an ancestor".

Some people also mentioned historical changes in the interpretation of dream symbols, especially changes brought about by different Churches:

> When I went to school, there was a kind of common knowledge about dreams. For example, if you were not yet married and you dreamed you had sex with a certain girl, it was presumed that the dream showed you whom to approach. It was prompting people to enter into relationships with one another. Today, if you dream you have sex with a girl, it means you have a spiritual wife, a demon, and people bring themselves to deliverance services to be prayed

over for this demon to be cast out. Again, when you dreamt of a white snake, it could be a positive sign, even a blessing. But today it always means you have a demon. This comes from the new Pentecostal Churches: they have changed the way we look at dreams. Guidance from the ancestors was seen as a blessing in the past; today it is seen as something demonic. (Charles Chirwa, Chilenje)

Placing dreams in the context of life

In the past, we were told, a dream was placed firmly within the life-context of the dreamer. The life-context included his/her family, living and dead, plans and aspirations, relationships with others, and his/her moral conduct. The moral conduct was often the first focus of inquiry, since moral life provides or breaks the vital links with the ancestors:

When you brought a dream to the elders, they would first look at your moral conduct. They would ask you what you have done and what you are up to. They would ask you: "tawalufyenye?" (Did you not do some wrong?) It was after finding out where you went wrong, that they went to the lufuba (ancestor spirit shrine) to ask the ancestors for mercy. And they knew ways how to discern whether the ancestors accepted or not. (Mr Bernard Mubanga, Kabwata)

Concerning the dreams themselves, we traced two interesting principles of discernment: focusing on the mood of the dream and on the ending of the dream:

When you saw a person, an ancestor, or a lion, or something else in the dream, the first thing the elders asked you was: "How did he look? Was he angry? Or was he happy?" When he was happy, this meant a confirmation: the ancestors told you: "you are on the right track". To see a happy ancestor meant a blessing. To dream of a snake or a lion or another fierce animal in a joyful setting could also be a blessing. Such animals were seen to be linked with the ancestors of the chiefs – when such dreams occurred in a posi-

tive mood. Because in the past there were lions who were [departed] chiefs. To climb a mountain in a joyful mood could mean that you are overcoming a problem.

A sad or angry mood, or an angry face, showed you that there was something wrong. The elders would ask you to examine yourself. Maybe you did something wrong. In the past we were not hiding things from the elders; we would tell them the truth. Maybe I stole something. Maybe I committed adultery. There was no point in hiding things, since the dreams themselves were revealing such things. The ancestor is not happy. This dream needs attention. You must do something. Sometimes it meant to go to the shrine and offer libation. Sometimes it meant to perform a ritual hunt to test the will of the ancestors. Sometimes it meant to look after orphans or the elderly or people whom you had neglected.

The ending of a dream was also important. A good ending was a good sign and an encouragement. If you were fighting with a person but at last you overcame him, it meant you would overcome the person whatever he tried to do. But if he overpowered you in the dream, or if the chasing animal brought you down, then there was need for action in your life. Sometimes it meant that you were with a cibanda [the shade/spirit of a dead person, usually of an-other family]; you had to wash your hands and your feet in medicines. If you were given food to eat in the dream, it was a sign of witchcraft. You needed to vomit, and vomit-ing was induced in the morning when you woke up. If you fell down in your dream, it could mean that you had to take extra care in what you were doing; things may be more dangerous than you think. If a woman was raped in a dream, it meant that a witch was having sex with her while she slept. Such dreams we brought into the public. We would send people to the house of the witch at dawn or at dusk, who announced throughout the village that "we know the witches who are doing this". Thus it was hoped that the witch would stop such evil behaviour. A bad ending *in a dream usually meant that something needed to be done upon waking up." (Mr Bernard Mubanga, Kabwata)*

Dreams thus could give subtle guidance: Looking (1) at the mood in the dream (the mood of the different actors), (2) at the ending of the dream, and (3) at the different characters present in the dream, one could find orientation about which people or families to approach or which relationships to mend or to break. Mood and ending provided insights into the points of crisis that needed attention and action.

Dreams and the nature of the human person

How one makes sense of dreams depends much on the implicit understanding of human nature. The following reflections are based on remarks of various elders; though they came from different cultural backgrounds (Bemba, Nsenga, Chewa), they brought dreams into contact with very similar questions of life.

a. Dreams and family

When you dream, you are close to your family. If you are far away from the family, you will see each other in dreams. And you should see one another, because you are of the same family. (Mr & Mrs Zulu, Chilenje)

A person in Zambian traditions is primarily and essentially related to his/her family / kin. One cannot conceive of the human person in isolation from his/her family, whether family is found on the matrilineal side, on the patrilineal side or on both lines. There is a spiritual connection between family members, both the living and the dead, which shows itself in many traditions, in many religious concepts and experiences, from birth to death and beyond. It shows itself also in dreams.

Also today, a number of people could recall for us dreams that announced important family events:

I dreamt of coffins, and the next day I was told that my sister had died.

I dreamt of my son: windows were breaking and a lot of broken glass was on the floor. I woke up, sweating and my heart pounding, and I knew instantly that my son was not ok. I phoned, and I was told that my son was stabbed in an armed robbery. Fortunately, he survived.

In the past the spiritual connection between family members was taken for granted; we were told that dreams were expected to reveal important family matters. As one person put it:

At the time of my late grandfather, there was no telephone. But he did not need a telephone. A dream would reveal to him if a family member was sick or if he/she died. He would travel back to the family on account of a dream, just to find people on the way with a message, saying: "you have a funeral". But he knew it already because of the dream. (Kaniki Kafupi, Mpeshi)

b. Dreams and the ancestors

When you sleep you are close to death and to the dead. (Mr Banda, Bauleni).

Many people compared dreaming with death. By falling asleep one experiences something of death and comes close to the dead. Dreams are an open window to the world of the dead: you may enter into their world, and the dead also may enter into your world.

This is true especially for the ancestors. The intrinsic connection and communion with the ancestors in dreams was something one could expect to happen; in difficult times of uncertainty, sickness and death, a visit of an ancestor could be anticipated. Especially during the precarious time of pregnancy, guidance from the ancestors in dreams was expected to come. A relative of the expecting couple would dream of a deceased kin, who wanted to be named into the new child, and such dreams were usually followed. Here a contemporary example (from Bauleni compound):

Dream: naming children after my grandparents
We made an involuntary experiment with dreams. My niece was pregnant with twins: a boy and a girl (ba mapasa). I

dreamt of my own grandfather and grandmother. When the twins were born, I narrated the dream to my niece and expected her to name both children after my grandparents. Now, in order to please me, they named the girl after my grandmother, but for the boy they took a name from the husband's side. The result is that the girl today is leading a very successful life and has become an important person in society. But the boy has been messing around ever since childhood and has never come to achieve anything. That is why we know it is important you name your child after the dream that is received.

Beyond such general expectations of certain dreams to happen at certain occasions, many of the people whom we interviewed could give us very personal examples of dreams in which their ancestors intervened into their lives at specific times with an important message. Some of the ancestral dreams were related with the concerns of sickness and healing:

Dream: my grandfather calls me out of hospital
I was very sick in hospital in Katete. My grandfather came to me in a dream and commanded me: 'tomorrow morning you leave the hospital, otherwise you will die'. The next morning I explained to the doctor that I was leaving the hospital. So, I was discharged. Back in the village, my grandfather came back to me in another dream, and told me to go to a certain village. The next day, just when I was about to leave for that village, a certain man (a tailor from Tanzania) came to me from that very village and told me: 'I had a dream about you: I was told to show you a certain tree, a Chipelembe *tree, and take the bark from the Western side of the tree, and soak the bark in water for you to be cured.' We went together to the bush and with just one piece of bark from one tree soaked in water that I drank I was completely cured. (Mr Banda, Bauleni)*

Authority figures within the family who have established a certain relationship with a child could remain close to the person also after death:

Dream: my grandfather warns me to fear snakes

When I was a child, my grandfather took me aside, and said: "We have chosen you in our family. I will give you medicine so that no snake can harm you." He made incisions into my body. When I came home, my grandmother told me: "Since you have received this medicine, from now onwards you are not allowed to add salt (umucele ubishi) to your food once it is cooked". These instructions were strictly followed in our family, and I was never allowed to add salt to my cooked food. One day I was bitten by a green mamba (ngoshe). The other children ran back to the village saying that I had died. But my grandfather was relaxed: "Francis cannot die through a snake-bite!" Indeed, I remained unharmed by the snake in spite of being bitten. Now, when I entered boarding school, I had a dream. By then my grandfather had died. He came to me with a warning: "From now on, you have to be afraid of snakes". I woke up, and tried to make sense out of the dream. Why should I start fearing snakes, since I had received the medicines against snake bites? So, I asked myself whether I had followed our taboo of not adding salt. I inquired from my friends, and they admitted: "Yesterday, when we ate, while you were away, we added salt onto the relish, and you ate from it not knowing what we did." Then I knew that my grandfather had come to warn me in the dream that from now onwards the medicines in my tattoos had lost their power. (Mr Mupinde, Kabwata)

Dream experiences like the above are treasured, remembered, and retold, and thereby the dreamer's own identity is built up in relation to the identity of an important ancestor.

In the past, dreams were but one sphere out of many that concerned a person's relationship with the ancestors. Ancestors guided the ritual hunts; they could be invoked in a number of divination systems, were present in naming ceremonies, at rites of passage, hunting expeditions, beer brewing, iron smelting, pot-burning, (all such activities were guarded by specific taboos) and of course in the extended funeral traditions; all important aspects of life were woven together into a comprehensive set of experiences of communion with the ancestors, of which dreams were but a part.

Today, the ancestors have been "dethroned" from such a central place. Some Churches have demonised the ancestors. This plays itself out also in relation to dreams. Many people do not know whether to follow the promptings of an ancestor or not. One active member of the Catholic Women's League reported recurring dreams of her late grandmother (who had been a traditional healer):

> **Dream: my grandmother calls me to become a healer**
> *I dreamt a number of times of my late grandmother. She came to show me medicines in the bush: trees and roots, so that I should start to cure people. She would show me what to do. But in another dream she became demanding and commanding: I should buy white beads and a white dish for her. She said I was chosen to become her successor.*

The dreams frightened the woman: she did not want to follow into the footsteps of her grandmother to become a traditional healer. She felt it stood in opposition to her Christian life and she made the decision to disregard her dreams.

c. Dreams and the soul

In dreams, we were told, we see things *mu mupashi* (*mu mzimu*) –"in spirit". The active part of a person during dreaming is his/her *mupashi* (Bemba) or *mzimu* (Nyanja), terms which refer (sometimes simultaneously) to different spiritual aspects or realities. The terms refer to a person's own spirit or soul. They also refer to the person's basic character, good or bad. They refer to the guardian spirit/soul of an ancestor (for example whose name one has been given, or inherited). The terms also refer the family ancestors, and in a wider sense to spirits associated with past and present peoples, and with the land. *Mu mupashi* (*mu mzimu*) refers also to the spiritual world at large.

Rather than trying to neatly separate the different meanings of *mupashi* or *mzimu* with clear boundaries and identities, one may also try to see in the fusion of different realities the expression of a connected "self", a connected soul, which is both individual and communal. The human soul has an essential connection with the spiritual world, especially with the ancestors of one's family. My ancestors can act on my soul and also speak through my soul. Dreaming is not seen as some sort of solitary exercise; when one dreams, one is not alone.

This understanding of the soul – being autonomous, while essentially also connected to others and to the spiritual world at large – captures well a universal experience of dreaming: In dreams, I am both active and passive at the same time. While I have a personal identity in my dreams with my own willpower and mind, I am simultaneously acted upon by others, mostly beyond any possibility of controlling the events. The settings/ sceneries/ objects and actors of the dream change beyond my own control and so do my own motives and undertakings in the dream. I am acting and acted upon at one and the same time. Dreams happen not just on the dreamer's initiative, but equally on the initiative of the spiritual world to which one is related. The dreaming 'self' is a meeting point of multiple actors.

d. Dreams and the rhythm of life

In the past the elders distinguished different types of dreams. There were dreams dreamt at the beginning of the night. They digested what you had experienced during the past day. If you had thought much about something during the day, it would come back to you at the beginning of the night. Such dreams were not seen to be important. Then there were dreams towards the end of the night. They showed you what you would be busy with the next day. Again, such dreams were not seen to be very important. Then there were dreams that were dreamt in the middle of the night. Such dreams were regarded as important. In the middle of the night one was close to death. In such dreams one was close to the dead ones. The soul travelled and visited. One could meet "in spirit". And the ancestors could speak to you. Dreams dreamt in the middle of the night were regarded as important. (Mr. Mubanga, Kabwata)

Immersions into the spiritual world are not continuous, but structured by the times of day and night, be it understood in the literal or in a metaphorical sense. There are times when one is closer to the spiritual realm, or where the spiritual realm impacts itself with greater force. This can be, for example, in the middle of the night. The "middle of the night" is sometimes taken in a literal sense of referring to some clock-time, say 01:00 – 03:00 AM. The "middle of the night" stands more often as a metaphor for closeness to death, to the ancestors, and to the surrounding spiritual forces. The "middle of the night" is a time of danger: when the witches are active, and when demons and spirits may cause havoc. "Satanists" in urban Zambia are said to meet at such times. But the middle of the night is also seen as the time of closeness to the ancestors and to God. Today, many Christian Churches stress the importance of overnight prayers, as well as the importance of waking up to pray in the middle of the night: both to defeat the powers of darkness, and to experience closeness to God, where special revelations can be received. In the middle of the night one is close to the spiritual world.

The mode of being-in-the-world is not continuous, but follows a structured rhythm. In many rural Zambian cultures, one may find a parallel or an analogy in the structure of the "hot" and "cold" spheres of life (the *mdulo* in Chewa), where "hot" spheres may refer to the productive and cultivated village life of adult living, while the "cold" spheres link up to the forest, wild animals, to the ancestors, and the dead. "Hot" and "cold" spheres are separated from each other, should not mix, each coming with its own mode of being-in-the-world, for example sexually active periods in the hot spheres, and abstinence in the cold spheres. Yet only the rhythm of both together constitutes productive reality. Similarly, the rhythm of day and night, waking life and sleep, brings along different, but complementary experiences of being-in-the-world: the day focuses on the activities of the physical body, while the night is marked by the actions in the spiritual realm, where the physical body is passive. Being-in-the-world follows the rhythm of life and death; the complete and healthy human person is fundamentally understood as being in union with the realm of both the living and the dead.

This rhythm is marked also by appropriate taboos: communion with the spiritual world follows certain rules and is not something just to be taken for granted. In the past it was by following the culture, the traditions, that one could ensure the blessings and helpful dream interventions of the ancestors when one was in need. To be blessed with certain dreams, one needed to follow the correct cultural procedures (*ukwenda mu ntambi*). Here an example from the Luapula Province, (Yongolo, at the edge of the Bangweulu Swamps).

Dream: finding the body of Paul

*One of our relatives drowned in the Luapula River. We were looking for his body, but could not find it. We found his canoe at the bottom of the river with his fishing nets, but nothing of the body. Usually bodies of drowned people come up after three days. But more than five days passed by, and we kept on searching for the body in vain. I knew that we were searching in vain, because we were neglecting our traditions (*ntambi). Since I was a headman, I asked the clan in charge on that stretch of the river for the* kupu-pa *(ritual prayers) to pray to the ancestors. They threw white flour and prayed. The Church choir at the funeral house had been busy singing songs. A knowledgeable woman from across the lake approached me and told me that in our tradition we should not sing funeral songs until the dead body is found. I consulted with other elders who agreed with the woman; then I stopped the choir from singing. I also instructed the youths who were searching for the body to remove their shirts. In our tradition you should not wear shirts when you search for a person who has drowned. At night we slept. I dreamt a dream: Paul [the dead person] came to me and said: "I am not there where you are looking for me" and then I saw exactly where the body was hidden. Another person present at the funeral house also dreamt the same dream. Short before dawn he woke up and said: "I have dreamt where our brother is." I also said "I dreamt where the body is!" The two of us together lead the search party to the spot we had dreamt about. It was far away from the spot where we had located the boat. Under the papyrus and floating islands we found the remains of the body that were left by the crocodiles: the* *head and the shoulders, which we then buried. (Chisasa Muchengwa, Yongolo).[6]*

In the past one needed to follow the traditions to allow a mode of being-in-the-world that brought contact with the ancestors. While the ancestors today have lost much of their importance, the underlying logic remains the same; one needs to cultivate a certain way of life, at least temporally, in order to enter into a special relationship with the spiritual world. Many *ng'angas* and also members of the Zion Churches cultivate their relationships with the spiritual world by observing taboos and rules. In urban Zambia, many Christians prepare themselves for extraordinary experiences with God by prolonged times of fasting and prayer. Though it is maintained that God can speak at any time, the closeness to God is maintained by means of a structured life of fasting and prayer, through which one maintains a special mode of being-in-the-world. In Bauleni, a number of pastors used extended periods of prayer and fasting during the founding period of their Churches, and claimed that in such times they were blessed with extraordinary revelations in their dreams.

e. Effects of dreams on body and soul

When a woman is raped in her dream, it means she has been raped. In the past we would bring the culprit to court and he would be punished. Some people use medicines to sleep with women as if in a dream. What happens in a dream happens to you. When you dreamt you were given meat to eat, it meant that somebody tried to bewitch you. Upon waking up you needed to vomit. People would make you vomit what you ate in a dream. In case one dreamt of having wrestled throughout the night with someone, which could mean that one is being followed by a cibanda *(the "ghost" or "shade" of a dead person), one needed to wash ankles and hands in medicines. At home we used the roots*

---

[6] Unfortunately, this dream of Chisasa Muchengwa was later taken as evidence by the family that he was involved in witchcraft. How could he have such knowledge? He became accused to be a *cisanguka,* a human crocodile, who had killed the man who drowned. He was expelled from the village. Meanings of dreams are contested: what one person claimed as knowledge derived from a dream in consequence of following cultural practices, was seen by others as engagement in witchcraft.

of the Musamba-mfwa (a Cassia) *and* Kasongole (Strychnos cocculoides) *trees. Upon waking up after a bad dream, we washed hands and ankles: this was a usual thing to do after a bad dream.* (Mr & Mrs Zulu, Chilenje)

How frightening such an experience can be, may be shown in the following example (collected in Chilenje):

When my uncle bewitched me, I dreamt that my hand was changing into the paw of an animal. When I woke up, I went to a priest, who told me I should not worry. "It is just a dream." I tried not to worry. But when I looked into the mirror I could see a shadow over me and I knew that what happened in the dream was happening to me. Many things have been happening in my family. They are not normal and they announce themselves in our dreams.

Where people look for help to neutralise bad dreams, solutions are offered along different lines: one traditional healer of Bauleni simply recommends the chewing of some leaves of the *Mupundu* tree (*Parinari curatellifolia*) as a remedy against dreams in which one is given food to eat – a clear sign of witchcraft. Another healer suggested a more elaborate treatment to neutralise the effects of dreams that reveal spiritual harm, requiring a bath (if possible at a crossroad) with a mixture of an early-sown type of millet (*amale ya mwangwe*, which is white and said to be a sign of blessings and good luck), the bark of the *Munganunshi* tree (*Acacia polyacantha*, which has a strong smell and is used also to wash away evil spirits as well as keeping away snakes from the house), and a creeper that crosses a road (*mupindwanshila*) – so as to block bad luck in the same way as the plant cuts through the road. Another person whom we interviewed followed the advice of his father after recurring bad dreams, and since then keeps a powder made of the *Ndale* tree (*Swartzia madagasariensis*) ready in his house:

In the morning after a recurring bad dream I was told to place the powder into a cup and place the cup on my head. Then I was supposed to take a burning coal with a spoon and drop it into the cup on my head. With the sound of the extinguishing fire I was supposed to place the cup slowly on the ground and go back into the house without looking backwards. Later on I was told to empty the cup on the rubbish heap. The dream did not come back. (Albert Muntoya, Kasamba Parish, Luapula)

That concrete bodily actions need to be taken as protective measures against the spiritual and physical effects of dreams is acknowledged today in some Churches, where affected body-parts need to be anointed with holy oils. While actions taken in the spiritual world affect the physical body, correct actions taken on the physical body also affect or correct its spiritual aspects.

Also vomiting is induced in some Churches. This can be done in reaction to dream experiences (especially after dreaming to be given food to eat) or to other manifestations that show that the body or soul is being manipulated and stand in need of deliverance. One pastor induced vomiting in his clients after periods of fasting by making them drink a blessed mixture of olive oil, milk and salt; in a Zion-type Church we witnessed that vomiting was induced by drinking a mixture of holy water and ashes. In a number of deliverance sessions of different Churches people started to vomit spontaneously while being in a trance on the floor, which we interpreted as an (unconscious) desire to get rid of negative spiritual objects and powers that threaten the life (or the success) of the person.

Conclusion

In the past as in the present, many people understand themselves (and construct their 'selves') in relation to important dreams. This has brought the question of dreams into the context of a wider understanding of the human person and his/her fundamental relation to the world. To deal with dreams demands to engage with such fundamental questions that concern human nature and especially the intrinsic impact of relationships on the human soul.

Many Western psychological approaches to dreams are essentially inward-looking and reflexive: my dreams, by means of powerful symbols, can teach me something about my own repressed wishes and drives (Freud), about neglected or supressed aspects of my personality (Jung, Perls), about my individual creative problem-solving powers that may be blocked by pathologies, psychic compensations or safe-guarding tendencies (Adler), about the format and structure of my long-term or semantic memories (Penfield) or about other issues that concern my inner life or different biological necessities. In Zambian approaches, important dreams rather point towards real people: The woman, for example, who dreamt of her late grandmother calling and commanding her to become a traditional healer, understood the dreams as a real meeting place with her grandmother, not as a con-coction of symbols about her own inner life, wishes or conflicts.

In the effects of dreams on the soul and the body, one finds another mark of difference from Western and also from traditional Christian understandings of dreams. In the early Christian Church, influential writers such as John Chrysostom and Tertullian argued that dreams in themselves do not affect changes in body and soul; unlike the effects of events experienced during waking life, the effects of a dream on soul and body evaporate together with the memories of the dream. This understanding of dreams as elaborated in Patristic times became part of mainstream theology (see the previous chapter).

This opinion of the early Church is not reflected in many Zambian ap-proaches, where dreams are seen to affect the self, body and soul. It could be argued that many new Churches today are successful in Zambia with their emphasis on overnight prayers, fasting, the im-portance of anointing of contaminated body-parts, holy waters, or induced vomiting, because such practices correspond to a worldview where the spiritual world impacts itself (positively and negatively) especially in the experiences of dreaming, leaving real marks and ef-fects in the body of the dreamer. The mainstream Churches cannot offer much help here, since they do not see a need for it.

One may ask the question whether such practices liberate people from the effects of their dreams or whether they induce in the long run more fear and alienation, creating the need for ever more elabo-rate rituals to neutralise bad dreams. Having said that, it remains ab-solutely necessary for mainstream Churches to engage positively with the worldview concerning human nature that underpins Zambian approaches to dreams. If not, answers to dreams may remain on a level that is of little concern to the persons who actually experienced them.

Bibliography

Chaplin, J. H. (1958). A Note on Central Africa Dream Concepts. *Man, 58*, 90-92.

Lanternari, V. (1978). Dreams and Visions from the Spiritual Churches in Ghana. *Paideuma, 24*, 85-102.

Mumbi, P. M. (2010, January). *Is it a healing contest? The Devil must be on the run: Some ethnographic notes.* Retrieved June 5, 2012, from fenza.org: http://www.fenza.org/docs/mum/is_it_a_healing_contest.pdf

Niehaus, I. (1995). Witches of the Transval Lowveld and their Familiars: Conceptions of Duality, Power and Desire. *Cahiers d'Etudes Africaines, 35*(138/139), 513-540.

Reynolds, P. (1992). Dreams and the Constitution of Self among the Zezeru. In M. Jędrej, & R. Shaw, *Dreaming, Religion and Society in Africa* (pp. 21-35). Leiden: Brill.

Storrs, A. E. (1995). *Know your trees.* Regional Soil Conservation Unit.

Sundkler, B. (1960). *The Christian Ministry in Africa.* London: SCM Press Ltd.

Sundkler, B. (1961). *Bantu Prophets in South Africa.* London: Oxford University Press.

Udelhoven, B. (2009). *Cases of Satanism.* Retrieved June 5, 2012, from fenza.org: http://www.fenza.org/docs/fingers/cases_of_satanism.pdf

Udelhoven, B. (2010a). *The Changing Face of Christianity in Zambia: Churches of Bauleni Compound.* Retrieved June 5, 2012, from fenza.org: http://www.fenza.org/docs/ben/changing_face.pdf

Udelhoven, B. (2010b). *Prophecy in Zambia.* Retrieved June 5, 2012, from fenza.org:
http://www.fenza.org/docs/ben/prophecy_in_zambia.pdf

BERNHARD UDELHOVEN

5

Zambian dreams and Western psychology: towards a pastoral approach

Bernhard Udelhoven

A dream of Grace

Grace, a middle aged woman living in Lusaka, dreamt she was sweeping her house. When she looked up (in her dream), she saw her mother coming towards her, as if she wanted to greet her. She was happy to see her mother and looked for a chair so mum could sit down. (Her mother was living abroad for a long time, and it had been long for mother and daughter to see each other). When she turned around with a chair, the mother was gone. She woke up, with a feeling that mum had come to greet her. The next morning she received a phone call, saying that mum had died.

Grace is a Catholic prayer guide and a psycho-social counsellor trained in different psychological models of making sense of dreams. From psychology she knew that dreams teach symbolically about the dreamer's own inner life, about her desires, anxieties, hidden wishes or conflicts. While she was quite aware of her inner wish to see her mother again, she felt that she was not doing justice to her dream if it was understood by introspection alone. She had literally seen her mother, not as a symbol, but in a way that was as real for her as a physical visit. She knew that there is an inner connection between her own life and the life of her mother. For Grace the dream was rooted in the wish of her mother to say good bye to her. Mum had come to make her strong for the time of mourning and she would continue also after death to support her. In fact, the whole family drew strength from the dream and it helped them to stay united after the funeral. A few years later, while Grace was in a difficult situation, she saw in another vision (in daylight) her mother coming towards her – in much the same way as she had dreamt, with a happy and peaceful face. As she looked for a chair for mum to sit down, the vision disappeared. Another confirmation for Grace: "Mum is still with us!"

Sharing her dream experience with other counsellors during a workshop on dreams, nearly each person present could tell of similar experiences of dreams that announced deaths or illnesses within their families. Introspection alone, they felt, was not doing justice to such dream experiences. Many of the counsellors took for granted that

- significant dreams origin in real inner connections between family members;
- dreams open up a person to different spiritual forces.

Western psychological approaches, they felt, were not able to deal with such important dimensions of dreams. At the same time, such interpersonal dimensions to dreams could also be very fear-provoking and give rise to many suspicions. Grace's dream was very consoling and strengthening. Other attendants of the workshop shared "bad dreams" of spiritual interpersonal encounters with witches that made people wake up with compelling questions: Which actions need to be taken? Which relationships need to be cut? Who is threatening me? Why?

Ordinary dreams, people felt, could be dealt with by Western psychological models. But when it came to ground-shaking inner experiences in extraordinary dreams, people looked towards Zambian cultural approaches for meaning, where the forces of the ancestors, but also of witchcraft, of spells, and of shades or ghosts are acknowledged.

When "bad dreams" occur, many people seek help. Where to go to depends on the question to which one seeks answers:

- "My dream points at a spiritual problem" (ghosts, demons, spiritual spouses, etc.). I will seek help from a Church or from a traditional healer known to be dealing with such issues.
- "My dream shows that somebody tries to harm me" (witchcraft). I will seek help from a traditional healer or from a Church that can give protection.

- "My dream shows that there are personal issues in my life that I need to deal with." I may seek help from somebody trained in psychology or speak things over with a friend who knows my situation.

Such options are often seen as mutually exclusive. A bad dream is either caused by a demon or by witchcraft or by an inner conflict. In the last instance the dream is often given little importance and may as well be ignored. Many pastors in Zambia deny that psychology can deal with spiritual problems ("spiritual problems need spiritual solutions"); insights from psychology are seen as non-applicable and irrelevant where a dream reveals witchcraft or demons. When dreams become true or reveal images that seem to apply clearly to a given situation, they are easily seen as "proof" to reveal spirits, ancestors or witchcraft at work.

In contrast, somebody trained in memory studies or interested in neurobiology would tend to look for natural explanations of such dream experiences and often succeed to find them: Precognition, premonitions and dreams that become true are often explained by referring to the multi-faceted nature of dreams and dream symbols, which makes it easy to relate a dream to many different subsequent life-situations. Psychology is well acquainted with our memory biases, suggesting that we remember accurate dream predictions, but forget easily the inaccurate ones, and retrospectively tend to make a dream narrative fit a subsequent life-experience. Psychologists also knows of overlaps of short-term and long-term memories and even of false memories, which can all play in favour of recalling dreams (in hind sight) that have become true. "I dreamt exactly what happened!" Once natural explanations are found, many dismiss the cultural approaches to dreams as false, not up to date or superstitious.

Such an exclusive "either – or" approach suffers from rejecting valuable insights from "the other side" that could make dream work relevant to the cultural setting while also being psychologically sound.

Culture and psychology

Psychology, as the study of the mind, looks at dreams in relation to the dreaming person's inner life, conscious or unconscious. The inner life copes and juggles not only with the needs and demands of the body, but unfolds to a great deal in relation to the perceived demands and expectations of significant persons and the community at large, which impinge constantly on my way of being-in-the-world. The social and cultural environment imprints on the person language, symbols and concepts, values and also fears. This affects also the dreams I dream.

For any dream there is more than one possible way of dealing with it, and people are aware of multiple and often conflicting ways for making sense of their dreams. On one hand the dreamer him/herself decides or sees which interpretation is fitting or not. But once a dream is shared or narrated it becomes a "social fact" and public knowledge. A shared dream is no longer a private dream; it has already transcended the scope of psychology. In the words of Johannes Fabian, "psychology is concerned with dreams as internal experiences, reflections of the subconscious. But 'dreams' as intentional messages, i. e. culturally defined means of communication, are the domain of anthropology."[1]

In the process of sharing a dream, diverse and multi-vocal layers of dream action and dream symbols are pressed into a single and selective narrative, put in words and dressed with meaning that corresponds with the community's framework. The dreamer is interwoven in a community which also discerns the dreams in view of strange or thought-provoking events or misfortunes that stand in need of clarification. When a personal dream is brought into the public realm, it meets with public approval or disapproval and becomes part of a public contest for meaning.

In the past, dream interpretation was not just a personal or private affair but a task entrusted to the elders. One needed to be very well versed in cultural practice if one wanted to discern the meaning of a

---

[1] Fabian (1966), 560.

dream.[2] The elders looked at the context of the dream, at the dreamer's moral conduct, at relationships, at the family of the living and the dead and could place the dream in a much wider context than the youngsters. Dreams could establish lifelong relationships with a particular ancestor; they could initiate rules & taboos; they could guide the dreamer to the art of healing and the knowledge of medicines. They could also warn about inherent danger, cut redundant family relationships and guide life into new directions. Dreams had the power to transform the person's spiritual beliefs and even beliefs of the community.

When dreams become public, they become part of a complex way of forming individual and social identities that can legitimate and compel social action. Witches, for example, have been revealed and labelled so because of dream experiences of those who felt affected by their powers. Interplay develops between an individual's dream and the community's worldview, expectations, fears or suspicions, which – if appropriated by the dreamer – may be reflected back in future dreams, but which may also be rejected, or manipulated, in forthcoming dream narrations.[3] Psychological insights, if they want to be relevant, need to take account of the wider community, beliefs, insights and worldview.

Clash of paradigms

In the struggle to apply insights of Western psychology in a meaningful way to dreams in Zambian cultural settings, one should not forget that the different approaches to dreams developed within their own cultural climates and contexts, sustained through different practices and goals. Dominant psychological frameworks (for example psychodynamic, psychoanalytic, cognitive, or neurobiological theories) have their roots in Enlightenment cultures, where the spiritual world does not play a defining and causal role, can be ignored, eclipsed, reduced to other dimensions, or at times be even outright denied.

---

[2] One person mentioned yet another reason why dream interpretation was left to the elders: "Dreams reveal secrets. As one could dream about the secret deeds of an elder, the elders controlled what was made public and what was to remain secret." (Mr. Bernard Mubanga, Kabwata, 5 November 2011.)

[3] See Reynolds (1992) for different aspects of the public making of dreams.

Since psychology deals with subjective experiences, psychological approaches to dreams cannot be pressed into the scientific paradigms as maintained strictly by the natural sciences. Determining the meaning of dreams goes beyond an investigation of causes and effects; it is a discipline akin to the human sciences where one has entered the sphere of hermeneutics and interpretation. Still, as far as the discipline strives to present itself before a scientific background, it needs a solid objective basis for its analysis. Since inner states and psychological processes are not readily visible and objectively observable, they have been analysed in psychology in relation to the person's own explicit associations (Freud), the observation of a person's concrete behaviour (Skinner), or in relation to observations of changes in the human brain: for example the creation of new synapses between neural networks or the emission of stimulating chemicals. Concerning the latter point, the discoveries brought about in the scientific field of neurobiology within the last decades do not make it possible any longer to uphold a strict dualism between the mind (and spirit) on one side, and biological processes in brain and body on the other side, as if one has little to do with the other. Specific inner movements of the psyche can be linked today very concretely to specific measurable activities in the brain and vice versa. The whole inner world of subjective experiences, including dreams and thought, are tied to the biology of the brain; leading neurobiologists today affirm the dependency of the human mind and psyche on the biology of brain and body (Kandel, 2005).[4]

Affirming the achievements of neurobiology, however, does not lead necessarily to the conclusion that psychology reduces the inner life of a person to the world of biology. While the link created by a single synapse may be essential for a certain dream to be dreamt, it is not the single synapse which thinks or feels or dreams, but the human organism as a whole (Roth 2008). Going a step further, it is not the human organism, seen in isolation, which dreams, but the person,

---

[4] Kandel, who came originally from a psychoanalytic framework, won the Nobel Prize for showing concrete links between mental (conscious and unconscious) activities and neurobiological changes, leading to the consequent proposition that any psychological treatment needs to result in specific changes in the structure of the brain (for example the creation of new synapses or the blocking of old ones) if it wants to have any long-term effect.

who is fundamentally related to others and integrated into the wider cosmos, and, we may add, who is also open to the spiritual world.

It makes of course a difference if I see the origin and cause of a dream in the spiritual or occult world, or if I see dreams rooted in the biological processes in brain and body, where networks of neurons, synapses, stimulants and hormones produce experiences, feelings, memories, recognition and visualisations. The spiritual dimensions to dreams escape the specific focus of psychology. Theology, however, has long been acquainted with principles of multiple causalities on different levels, where grace (spiritual reality) and nature (physical, biological or empirical reality) are seen to be complementary rather than exclusive. The affirmation that spiritual life is intertwined with biological, psychological and social realities does not need to lead to reductionism from a theological point of view.

To reject the possibility of applying Western psychological insights to Zambian contexts would come close to an absolute cultural relativism and the rejection of a common humanity. Yet when trying to combine psychological insights and Zambian cultural insights, one should also pose the important question whether some dispositions and presuppositions situated in the Western world are carried forward in the process of applying psychology that go beyond the scientific paradigms, exporting cultural paradigms in disguise of science. In the Western world the human being is often (though not always) understood as an individual, striving towards autonomy, in a (largely) secularised and pluralistic world, where complex systems of law and economy build up and maintain individual boundaries. This view goes hand in hand with a strict dividing line between the objective outer world (shared by all) and the subjective inner world (particular to the individual person). This line, however, is not drawn so strictly in Zambia. Many Western psychological approaches to dreams were popularised in a climate where value is placed on a unique, complex and "authentic" interiority; psychology became a tool for finding an assumed or postulated "inner self" or "real self", be it as a holistic "Gestalt" (the perceived shape of its complete form) or in a composite form say of Freud's ego, super-ego and id, or other divisions. Especially feminist psychology has unmasked a number of Western cultural presuppositions that underpin psychotherapeutic practice.

O'Hara, for example, in her critic of Western psychotherapy, looked at the concept of the (assumed) 'inner self':

> *Participants in the process of psychotherapy in Western so-*
> *cieties, whether clients or psychotherapists, perceive and*
> *experience themselves ... as distinct, autonomous agents,*
> *separated from other individuals by a whole array of*
> *boundaries of identity. Whether as the European self, full of*
> *dangerous tensions between aggressive and sexual drives*
> *barely contained by the rational will, or as the American*
> *self, enthusiastic, achievement-oriented, and transcending*
> *its animal baseness through hard work and religious com-*
> *mitment, Western modernist society has valorized individu-*
> *al experience and has placed at its center a monadic, de-*
> *contextualized person who is virtually unencumbered by*
> *any a priori external constraints.* [5]

Psychological approaches at large see in dreams projections coming from the person's inner world; dreams teach me something about my own complex inner life. For Freud, dreams were the royal road to the knowledge of the unconscious activities of the mind. Such a view removes the dreamer a step (or even several steps) from the immediacies of a dream: everything I dream about is but a symbol that stands for something else. Freud taught that the manifest dream content hides the latent dream content of "real" significances that can be retrieved and made conscious if one analyses the dream symbols with reference to the dreamer's own free associations. The "real meaning" points inwards. Also Carl Jung taught that the persons and objects one dreams about represent different inner aspects of the dreamer, which in the dream appear as projections, and they are treated in therapy as such.[6] When Peter dreams about Paul, the dream teaches something about Peter, not Paul. Psychodynamic and psychoanalytic approaches regard dream images as a mirror, which may not always be very clear, but which nevertheless can provide the dreamer with powerful insights into his/her own hidden desires and wishes, anxieties, unresolved childhood conflicts, relationships to parents and to other significant people that have shaped and still de-

---

[5] O'Hara's (n.d.)
[6] For psychodynamic approaches to dreams, see Mentzos (2011), 73-79.

termine much of his/her conscious and unconscious activities. Where such approaches develop a Jungian twist, attention to dreams can lead to greater awareness for neglected aspects of one's personality; dreams can help a person to develop hidden talents and to tap creatively into unconscious forces for greater wholeness and self-actualisation.

Proponents of cognitive psychology (Calvin Hall, William Domhoff) follow a different approach by stressing the continuity between dreams and waking life: dreams reveal the "conceptual system" of the dreamer that determines also behaviour in waking life. Our behaviour is based on a cognitive framework, shaped from childhood through a system of concepts, scripts and schemes that determine our roles, self-conceptions, conceptions of family and of others, of the world, of impulses, prohibitions, penalties, problems, conflicts, and also our affects – the way we think and feel about different things. Dreams show visibly in dramatic and playful form what is invisible: our concepts through which we process reality and on which we base our actions. For the cognitive school, dreams do not reveal the nature of the "self" (nor of the world, of a problem or of a relationship, etc.), but the conceptions that the dreamer has about such issues. Dreams reveal whether the world is experienced as a home or as a wasteland desert, whether a parent is seen as a tyrant or as a benevolent and nurturing figure, whether one sees oneself as active or passive in regards to certain confrontations. Affects shown in dreams are the affects I encounter also in waking life when in comparable situations. Dreams reveal what is allowed and what is forbidden for the dreamer, how to feel when something is done or omitted. Since we have different (and often conflicting) concepts of the different identities that we construct, attention to dreams can reveal a whole series of complementary scripts and schemes through which we perceive reality and through which we act upon reality.[7] An outsider therapist can help the dreamer to realise that self-conceptions, or concepts of significant relationships, or attitudes towards impulses (sex, anger, aggression, appetites, etc.) as revealed through the dreams may not always be well adapted to the world the person lives in; dreams can show entrapments in the way we look at the world

---

[7] Hall (1953), Domhoff (2010).

75

and at ourselves. Positive changes in regards to maladaptive thinking can lead to positive changes in a person's affect (the way the person feels – and dreams – about events, persons or things) and subsequently to positive changes in the person's relationships and behaviour.

The approaches of such different psychological schools have in common that dreams are seen as projections coming from the dreamer's own inner life. In Zambian traditions, in contrast, important dreams are seen to be direct experiences with others. Dreams are authored by multiple agencies; they give knowledge that goes beyond the dreaming individual. People may engage with others in their dreams: with people, ancestors, spirits, ghosts, witches, and shades, in encounters that may even determine each other's future. In Zambia, important dreams point outwards, not inwards. This is not surprising if one considers that the human condition is not seen in isolation from relationships, from the collective, from the spiritual world, and from an essential interconnectedness of the dreamer with the ancestors, and in a wider sense with life-forces present in the whole universe. One cannot speak of an individual inner "self" in any absolute sense; the human soul is both individual and communal.

That dreams often arise from the inner struggles of an individual person, is also acknowledged in Zambian cultural traditions. But such dreams are not given much significance. Dreams are not analysed in regards to self-knowledge; what counts is knowledge about the true nature of relationships, about the real meaning of events, or about the future outcome of a person's endeavours. Dreams are not a royal road to the individual unconscious mind (introspection), but open up direct experiences with spiritual forces that can help him/her but that can also hinder and harm, which in turn are bound up with the person's concrete relationships. Such a view on dreams corresponds with a way of life and self-understanding, where human relationships are central and essential, but also complex and changing, where different obligations easily conflict with each other. Dreams are used not to discover an "authentic" interiority, but to renegotiate relationships.

As a consequence Western psychology seems to be answering questions about dreams that many people in Zambia do not ask, while leaving questions unanswered that are essential for people. The challenge for any meaningful pastoral approach to dreams that intends to be psychologically sound is to extend psychological insights to the concerns that are vital for people: relationships.

Meeting points

In the previous chapter I laid out how a number of traditional Zambian approaches to nightmares focused on the different moods in the dream and on the ending. Dreams with a bad ending, where the dream characters display a "bad mood" or an aggressive and angry disposition, need attention and action: one needs to do something about it.

It is not difficult to draw parallels to psychodynamic insights: moods in dreams help to discern the inner emotional states of the dreamer, and also help to link up the dream symbols to situations of waking life that trigger such moods. Endings of a dream are equally important: a dream can "wake you up" when dream actions run towards a conflict that the dream itself cannot solve; one wakes up with powerful symbols that may express the unresolved conflict. Sigmund Freud, for example, saw in nightmares the result of failure of inner dream work: a nightmare or anxiety dream occurs when the dream fails to disguise symbols and emotions which the dreamer tends to repress.[8] He suggested that a smooth dream protects sleep by creating a pleasant feeling of wish fulfilment out of inner and outer incentives, desires and stimuli; it tries to disguise stressors or conflicts that may lead to discomfort. Yet when the dream confronts the dreamer with insufficiently disguised but powerful repressed wishes, the dream experience becomes upsetting and turns into a nightmare. The nightmare points a finger at inner or outer conflicts that stand in need to be addressed. Freud saw in the dream experiences of nightmares mere projections of the unconscious; Zambian approaches see real encounters. Yet both share at least one common insight: important nightmares should not be neglected.

---

[8] Freud (1947 (1899)), 448-477.

We may ask the question, which psychological frameworks (beyond Freud) seem more promising when dealing with dreams in Zambian cultural settings? Humanistic and person-centred approaches (Carl Rogers) can naturally provide a good starting point for a counsellor who may not share the client's worldview. Though humanistic approaches are also rooted in a Western notion of the human individual (seen to have a natural drive towards self-actualisation, creativity and also own responsibility), they start with the client's own framework, recognising his/her unique social context, thereby giving room and respect for the cultural dimensions; the dreaming person is seen as the unique owner of the dream experience and therefore also in the driving seat for finding the dreams' meanings. The counsellor does not need to agree with the dreamer's framework, but he/she needs to respect it as the starting point. Nevertheless, through careful listening, empathy and encouragement, one can mutually give the process of finding meaning in the dream a certain direction that is sound also from a psychological and Christian moral point of view.

Especially the schools that enhance a vision of the human 'self' as being intrinsically relational (and not atomistic) seem promising to deal with dreams in the Zambian context. One may think for example of socio-cultural psychological approaches (Lev Vygotsky), of inter-subjective psychoanalysis (Heinz Kohut), of relational psychoanalysis (Stephen Mitchell), and also of feminist psychology which has deeply challenged the notion of an autonomous 'self'. In a marked contrast to Freud's thermodynamic model to psychology, such approaches see the primary motivations of the psyche (and by implication of dreams) in real relationships rather than in sexual or aggressive inner drives, fantasies or inner struggles and repressions. The existence of inner subconscious drives, struggles or repression is not denied in such approaches, but they are seen as firmly embedded in the context of the concrete relationships within which they arise. In such approaches a significant dream is always more than a personal issue: it puts a finger also on social tensions and in a wider sense even touches issues of justice and peace. It comes closer to Zambian traditional approaches to dreams, where a dream was analysed within a holistic setting where the soul of the dreamer is related to his family, living and dead, and to the life-forces of the whole cosmos.

Attempts to positively combine Western and Zambian approaches in a way that remains true and respectful to the different understandings of human life, start maybe by nature from a postmodern paradigm: building on assumptions of epistemological pluralism (meaning an awareness that no single theoretical framework can explain reality in its totality), different theoretical foundations – even when they seem to be mutually exclusive – are allowed to stand side by side so as to come to a fuller appreciation of reality. Yet a cultural relativism where one interpretation is as good as the other will not prove itself as practical or workable in a pastoral setting, where people expect answers and especially guidance in regards to their dreams. Choices need to be made. To recognise the validity of different cultural traditions besides each other therefore should not prevent us from questioning and also challenging entrenched worldviews and presuppositions that leave little space for positive growth in today's world. If Zambian approaches to dreams can challenge Western notions of the self (especially the individual, atomistic self), Western approaches should also be able to challenge Zambian notions, especially where dreams lead to severe suspicions and accusations, or where they stand divorced from self-critique and self-examination.

Pastoral agents who come in from a Christian angle should strive towards an understanding of dreams that allows for positive growth in relationships and in self-awareness. People approach priests, sisters and pastors with their dreams because they expect a Christian answer that nourishes their faith. Unfortunately, even in the Christian context dreams have been abused to identify Satanists, witches and evil intentions in other people who were unfortunate enough to appear in the dreams, increasing mistrust, avoidance and fears, instead of enhancing love, trust, humility, and the mutual up-building of relationships.

Before giving some examples of such positive dream work respectful to the cultural setting, I want to start the discussion about the Christian framework to dreams with an overview over theological approaches as practised in different Churches in Zambia.

Responses of different Zambian Churches to dreams

Christianity in Zambia, with a multitude of different Churches / denominations, is pluralistic. This applies also to approaches to dreams: different theologies stand side by side. In what follows I will present a brief sketch, outlining different frameworks that we encountered in different Churches about the question of divine dreams (dreams inspired by God) and dreams influenced by demons or witches. Note that the spectrum of different approaches does not neatly divide along denominational lines. Within a single denomination one finds often a number of different approaches side by side. Many pastors follow an improvised or "ad-hoc" approach to dreams rather than having a clear roadmap by which they are guided.

1. On one side of the spectrum are Churches and approaches which devalue dreams: dreams were revelatory only in Biblical times; since God has already revealed all he wanted to say in the scriptures, there is no need any longer to listen to dreams, except maybe in regards to questions of self-knowledge. Dreams are the realm for psychologists, not for theologians. Examples are the Jehovah Witnesses. This approach goes usually hand in hand with a theology of dispensations as elaborated by some evangelical Churches: Dreams were revelatory during certain periods and dispensations (for examples in the times of the Prophets, or in the time of the formation of the Biblical canon); the times of divine dreams are over, since they have found their fulfilment in Jesus Christ. Certain times of crisis, though, may provoke dispensations where dreams play again a major role in divine revelations, for example the dispensation of the "time of rapture" or of the "time of great tribulation". Apart from such extraordinary times, dreams no longer play a revelatory role in the lives of the faithful.

2. On the other side of the spectrum (examples are some African Initiated Churches, some *Mutumwa- / Mizimu-* type Churches, and also some newer Pentecostal Churches), dreams – like visions – play an important revelatory part; true prophetic value is attached to relevant dreams. Dreams are seen to have the potential to guide people through unclear situations with divine messages. Moreover, divine dreams, especially of the Church found-

ers, may have implications on Christian doctrines. The doctrines of some of the older African Initiated Churches in Zambia – an example is the Mutima Church (*Mutima walowa wa Makumbi*) – were laid out in references to dream experiences and visions of the founders. Also new Pentecostal Churches today can be open to such revelations. One Pentecostal pastor in Bauleni compound, for example, founded his Church with reference to a divine dream that revealed to him the name of God the Father and of the Holy Spirit. Such revelatory dreams, however, are often restricted to the founding members of the Church.

3. In many new Pentecostal Churches in Zambia, dreams and visions do not bring forth new divine revelations about Christian doctrines, but do have a lot to say about personal spiritual situations of members of the faithful or about people coming for help. Dreams (especially dreams of the pastors) are seen as prophetic and show that God is alive and guiding people through the pastors. Some people are called for prayers in response to the dreams of the pastor: "Tell so-and-so to come for prayers; I received a message for him/ her in my dream." Others bring themselves to pastors, prophets and "men of God" to receive personalised prophetic messages that the pastor received in dreams or visions.

4. Many denominations, especially mainstream Churches, hold prophetic dreams to be important, but also dangerous: as they can guide, they can also mislead. Dreams stand in need of interpretation. In a number of Evangelical Churches, the images of a dream need first to be compared with Biblical images, and the perceived message of the dream with the Biblical message – only then can one tackle the question about the origin of the dream and its role for moral guidance. Such thinking is based on the rationale that God continues to speak through dreams, but not in a sense that would contradict other parts of the Christian revelation. In other approaches the criteria of St. Paul (as laid out in 1 Cor. 12-14) are used: divine dreams are recognised by their fruits: whether they lead a person to Jesus Christ and bring peace and reconciliation, or whether they bring confusion and division. One does not, however, expect new divine revelations concerning Christian doc-

trines. In the Catholic Church, the distinction between private and public revelations (quoted in this book on page 41) acknowledges the reality of divine dreams that present a divine call to individuals or to the faithful at large in a certain period of time, while they cannot surpass or correct the revelation of which Christ is the fulfilment.

5. The following approach builds on approach number 4, yet does not follow strictly an "either-or approach" (supernatural versus natural origin of dreams). Instead, it affirms that God speaks potentially through all important dreams – since God is never absent from any significant human experience; God and the unconscious activities of the mind are seen as "co-authors" of an important dream.[9] Or with the words of St. Thomas Aquinas: "Grace builds on nature". Though God is not identical with the voices of the dream (a theological concept says that God is *transcendent*: meaning fundamentally different from creation, always going beyond our concepts and understanding, not able to be contained within the human fabrics of dream messages or other forms of human thought), he is nevertheless present in the dream and works *through* the natural processes of dreams rather than against them (a complementary theological concept says that God is *immanent*, meaning being present and working from within). This approach – looking at God to be transcendent and immanent at one and the same time – affirms that divine experiences in dreams are by nature infinite and wholesome and therefore cannot be limited to one angle or perspective alone (say a purely spiritual perspective) but touches always also psychological and social issues. This approach furthermore is not limited to "good dreams" (affirmative, healing, consoling); "bad dreams" also contain messages from God that can help a person to grow spiritually, make necessary decisions in life or rearrange one's worldview or self-image. The approach is quite open to Western psychology (often leaning towards a Jungian perspective). Here Western psychology has come to lead a rather peaceful coexistence with the Biblical and historical heritage – though one should not forget that it had taken many decades to grow to-

---

[9] An example would be Johnson (1989).

wards each other. The approach is also open to the new scientific insights of biology in regards to human thoughts and dreams, and seems fruitful when looking for an integral, trans-disciplinary and multi-dimensional framework.

Reactions of Churches to African spiritual forces

What can be said about African approaches, where (apart from God) also the ancestors, spirits, demons, and the forces of witchcraft may be experienced directly in dreams? The following approaches seem mutually exclusive:

1. Many approaches in Zambia across the denominational divide are well acquainted with such spiritual forces, which they expect to play a role in people's lives and dreams, but such forces are usually demonised: to follow the promptings of spirits that are distinct from God (like *ngulu* or *mashawe* spirits) is seen as leading a person directly into idol worship. A dream from God should be followed; a dream from other spirits and even from the ancestors should be discarded, also when it promises the gift of healing or the knowledge of medicines. Dreams that are seen as influenced by spiritual forces other than God himself need to be exorcised, cast out, or "neutralised" with holy oils, holy water, or acts of prayer: ultimately they will lead a person away from God.

2. The *Mutumwa* and *Mizimu*-type Churches tend to have a positive attitude towards spirits distinct from God. Though some demons and spirits with a negative influence need to be cast out, many spirits come from God and bestow special gifts on the possessed person. Initially such spirits tend to make the possessed person sick; once the name of the spirit is discerned and accepted (often in a *Mutumwa* or *Mizimu*-type Church), the sickness is cured or eased. The spirit now speaks to the person, often in dreams, bestowing special knowledge to the dreamer, who may himself/herself become a healer. To follow the promptings of such positive spirits (*mizimu*) is not seen as opposing the will of God, but a personal vocation one is duty-bound to follow: it is God who made the spirits and who sends the spirits; the rejection of this call leads to ultimate sickness or even death.

3. Approaches marked by Western Enlightenment thinking, in contrast, are often doubtful about the existence of spirits and find it difficult to accept that dreams reveal the anger or blessings of ancestors, witchcraft, demons, the future, the hidden unknown past, the death of a loved one, the required name for a new-born child, impending danger, or the location of a lost item (though such dreams are not foreign to the Biblical and theological heritage). Following the promptings of such dreams is seen not as idol worship (since the theologians do not really believe that such spirits actually exist) but as mere superstition.

Where theology develops strong agnostic attitudes or sheer disbelief towards African spiritual forces, people can find the answers of their Church irrelevant to their own problems; they do not feel understood in their personal and spiritual dimension. On the other hand, answers given by charismatic / newer Pentecostal approaches, where there is no hint of doubt about the existence of demons and spirits interfering in people's lives can in the long run increase a feeling of powerlessness and fear. Many people come to see themselves as eternal victims of spiritual forces and witches, always blaming others for their dream experiences, with no need for self-examination. Spiritual forces are linked so closely to relationships that people are easily excluded as witches or "Satanists" when they are associated with negative dream experiences.

Many new Pentecostal Churches that deal with the spiritual nature of a dream proceed with a spiritual or prophetic "diagnosis", a term borrowed from the medical field. As different pathologies in the medical field come with their specific cures (medicine against malaria is irrelevant for combating tuberculosis) so spiritual conditions also depend on a "spiritual diagnosis" for the discernment of the nature of the spirits that trouble the sleep of the dreamer. Demons need to be named if one wants to exercise authority over them. We find in Zambia today whole armies of "spiritual husbands", "demons from the sea-side", "demons from the mountains", "Satanic spirits", "generational family spirits", "anti-clockwise demons" and "spirits of confusions" (to mention but a few); new types of demons develop constantly, can be identified by their specific characteristics and come with their own way to be defeated through appropriate spiritual warfare. To deal with a demonic dream, it is believed, one has to deal with the demon – in the same way as "Coartem" is prescribed against malaria to any person irrespective of the individual background. The dreamer himself/herself is often seen (and often also wants to be seen) as a passive victim, unfortunately brought in contact with the demonic forces, often against his/her own will, through ignorance or through the malice of others.

As a result of such a "diagnosis", the spiritual realities are easily seen out of their cultural and personal contexts: they become reified and de-contextualised, as if the world of demons is a world apart with its own rules and behaviours in the spiritual world, which has little or nothing to do with the personal life-context of the dreamer. Bad dreams can be exorcised even though the pastor knows nothing of the family background, life-situation or history of the dreamer. The approach is demon-oriented, not person-oriented.

A person-centred approach versus of a demon-centred approach

A different, integral approach for dealing with cultural spiritual forces in dreams is also possible, and (I believe) healthier in the Zambian context. Thereby it is not necessary to make firm and clear assertions about the nature of the spiritual realities (the spirits in themselves) that appear in dreams or are discerned in dreams. Spirits, demons, or the effects of witchcraft are not denied, but remain always in the background of an analysis. Their life-context is more important. The approach is person-oriented rather than demon-oriented. One is aware that the impact of the spiritual reality is experienced in a personal way, different from person to person, depending on my own life-context and history.

The rationale behind this approach is that spirits (whatever their precise nature – spiritual and/or psychological and/or social) appear in dreams for a reason. Not just superficial reasons or "entry-points", that many Churches warn about in Africa (like eating contaminated food, tattoos, wearing contaminated clothes or using "demonic" cosmetics), but existential reasons that affect the core of a person: broken relationships, grave tensions in the family, traumas, guilt, expectations to which one cannot live up to, or a life lived in the context of permanent dishonesty or abuse of trust. Spiritual forces here cannot be neatly separated from the psychological and social contexts in which they appear. When the social and psychological contexts are addressed, one addresses (at least partly) also the spiritual realities, whatever their precise nature may be.

This thought is not foreign to traditional Zambian approaches to dreams, which have never upheld a strict separation of the spiritual world from physical and social processes; spiritual, social and physical worlds are interrelated and form one single reality. Again, where the human person is seen fundamentally as an interrelated being in a web of relationships with family & clan, with relevant people and ultimately with the whole cosmos, such interconnectedness and mutual determination should play itself out also in dreams. When the dream expresses this with the help of cultural concepts, then the logic of the traditional spiritual concepts can point at the issues and especially at the relationships that stand in need to be addressed.

Positive meaningful action upon a dream in this approach requires that the dreamer leaves the comfortable and passive role of victimhood and engages actively in the process of mending significant relationships. An example may be given. A married woman experienced recurrent dreams in which she was raped by another man, who remained in the dream but a shadow, escaping recognition. Two different traditional healers told her that men use certain forms of witchcraft to have sex with the women they admire while they sleep, pushing away the sleeping husband who is lying by the side. This was very plausible to her, and she did have some concrete suspicions about the culprit. But the woman was still left in doubt how to stop such experiences. A Christian counsellor advised wife and husband together to work on their actual relationship with one another, which was under many strains, instead of concentrating always on the unknown rapist. The mutual efforts towards each other made the dreams stop. Mutual forgiveness was part of their efforts. So were prayers. Her conclusion is that "whoever tried to rape me in my sleep, now he fails, because he needs to come in between myself and my husband, but we committed ourselves to tackle this together." Whatever or whoever caused the uncomfortable dreams, in the end the dreams helped to strengthen a relationship between spouses.

Had the woman resigned herself into victimhood, blaming others, it may have ended in a different way.

Whatever a dream may reveal about others, it is never independent of the movements of the dreamer's own heart. The demands and the calling of the Christian faith start always with one's own heart. Any "diagnosis" that opens a concrete way towards healing in this context points not at the demon or force of witchcraft, but on the demands of faith on relationships, on the level of forgiveness, on neglected duties within the family, on ruptures in social life, abuse of authority and other issues that prevent a wholesome and healthy communal life.

If one engages in addressing these issues in the context of faith, then the spiritual demonic aspects of dreams can be entrusted safely into the hands of God, beyond the worrying focus of the patient and the healer. It is surprising that the spiritual aspects themselves often point towards the broken relationships and neglected duties that stand in need to be addressed and healed. Some examples may illustrate this point.

Dream: my mother in a coffin

At one point in my life, I started to dream about my late mother. She was in a coffin, and we were body-viewing. All of us were very sad. I dreamt the same dream many times. The dream left me puzzled, and I went to ask an elder for the meaning. He asked me: 'When you looked at your mother in the coffin: who else was there at the coffin?' I said: 'There was also my niece, the orphan-daughter of my late brother. She was standing there at a distance and she also looked very sad.' The elder then asked me about this niece. I explained that she is kept by her mother's relatives, but that she is not well cared for. She does not even go to school. The elder told me: 'Your mother is telling you that you should care for your niece.' This prompted me to take my niece into our house, and to bring her to school. Since then the dream never came back. I know that my mother is happy with what I did.

The outcome shows that the elder approached the dream in a satis-
factory manner. The frequent dream occurrence stopped when the
perceived message of the dream was put into practice. The appearance of the late mother was seen by the elder in terms of the dreamer's relationships with the living family members that needed attention. A theologian or a psychologist may have argued with the elder
about the nature of the mother-figure in the dream. Can a dead person come back to give messages to the living? But if one leaves the
question about the precise nature of the mother-figure in the background, I believe, the solution offered by the traditional approach to
this captivating dream of amending relationships with the living family members remains compelling and ingenious. The Zambian approach of pleasing the spiritual world by loving the living finds reso-
nance in theology ("How can you love God whom you do not see and
hate your brother whom you see?") and also in relational psychology
where the 'self' and psychic forces are seen essentially in relation to
others.

From a psychological perspective one would say maybe that the
dream has chosen the best possible symbol to convey its message
and point at the broken relationships that the dreamer needed to
address in order to live a healthier life, also in the spiritual sense. The
dream chose the mother symbol as its key metaphor. In the matrilineal cultures of Zambia, which other symbol could have expressed
more powerfully the demands for unity and solidarity in the family,
and the care for the neglected niece with whom the dreamer was
related through the mother's side?

Dream: having sex with my late husband
*My husband died ten years ago. I went through the rite of
cleansing, yet never remarried. I live with some of my children. Five years ago my husband came back at night in my
dream to have sex with me. This dream came back repeatedly, up to a year ago. It was very disturbing. I loved my
husband, but the dead should not come back to you. I asked
priests to offer Mass for my husband. I approached the
Charismatics for prayers: it helped for some time, but then
the dream came always back. One day I shared my experiences with a friend. She asked me: "Do you go out with*

*men?" – "No", I said, "I have never been touched by a man
since my husband died". Then she asked "How do you go
along with your in-laws and the family of your late husband?" I said "At the beginning we went along well. They
cleansed me. Tensions came only five years ago, when the
ownership of the house was put on my name." My friend
asked me: "When did your late husband start coming back
to you?" Then I realised that it was the same time. My
friend advised: "You are with a* cibanda. *You have to sit
down with his family, otherwise it will not stop. Ask them
what they want from you." It was a very difficult step for
me. They said the house did not belong to me, but to them.
I explained that we had bought the house together. At least
we started to talk again. Though the issue of the house was
not resolved completely, the dreams stopped. I am free.*

Both women saw at the root of these dreams the cultural concept of
a *cibanda:* a shade or presence of the late husband, which comes as a
negative force, a burden that can bring madness and death. A widow
not yet cleansed (hence with a *cibanda*) is not allowed to marry outside the late husband's family or to engage sexually, else the *cibanda*
runs amok. Hence the first question of the friend, inquiring about her
sexual behaviour. Then the inquiry shifted successfully towards link-
ing the dreams to existing relationships with the in-laws.

A theologian and a psychologist might argue about the precise nature
of a *cibanda*. But one is not forced to put an answer to this question
into the foreground. The women looked at the dream experiences
not as encounters with an isolated ghost. The *cibanda* is firmly embedded in concrete relationships: very fragile relationships between
the remaining spouse (and her wider family) and the in-laws (and his
wider family), who were bonded together into a communal life of
defined relationships through the link of the husband, who is no
more. Embedded within the relationships are expectations about
sexual behaviour, possibilities of remarriage, questions of property,
and especially the future of the children.

Cleansing rites are part of the extended funeral rites. Most Churches
in Zambia have difficulties with such rites – not only because of difficulties with the spiritual notion that are implied, but also because of

injustices against the remaining spouse that can accompany the rites: accusations of having caused the death or of neglect. The mood of the family of the deceased can turn against the spouse, for whom the preparations for the cleansing rites (often already preceded by property grabbing and sometimes by beatings) can be very humiliating. Still, the cleansing rites constitute for many an important ritual that clarifies the relationship between the remaining spouse and the family of the late spouse. The threat of remaining with a *cibanda* becomes a mirror of this precarious relationship: not because the late husband has turned into an evil spirit, but because the relationship with his family is slowly but surely estranging: they were linked together through the husband who is no more. Remarriage outside his lineage, freedom for the woman, is possible only after the cleansing rites, when the remaining issues still in need to be addressed are clarified. In the above case, the issue of the house had not been settled, and the woman could not escape the *cibanda* that pointed towards and marked a broken relationship that needed clarification. Since it is the privilege of the kin of the dead to take control over the *cibanda,* the friend investigated about the existing relationships with the in-laws. Indeed, once a relationship was re-established by sitting down together, the *cibanda* disappeared. What could not be solved by prayers for the dead (looking at the *cibanda* purely as a spiritual force in itself) or by prayers of deliverance (praying for the troubled woman just by herself), was somehow addressed by the process of re-entering relationships with the family of her late husband.

The dream chose as key-symbol the late husband, coming as a *cibanda*, a spiritual force that belongs to another family, which cannot be appeased or integrated into one's own life without risking to become mad or to die. In a culture where the family of the husband is always from another clan, with its own spiritual forces to which one is not related – which other symbol but a *cibanda* could express better the hidden, unexpressed conflict with his family to whom one is no longer related?

Conclusion

Any meaningful interpretation of dreams has to link up with a person's experiences of being-in-the-world. Many people in Zambia experience themselves connected with the spiritual world that affects also their dreams. One does well to look at Zambian spiritual forces that play themselves out in dreams not in isolation from concrete relationships. The precise spiritual nature of such forces can remain in the background of an analysis. In the foreground stand the relationships to which they point and in which they actually arise.

Pastoral theology does not need to give the final answer about the nature of dreams. Instead, theology places any given answer into a wider picture: the dreamer's life-history, relationship with God, and relationships with others. When one responds to dreams by mending relationships or working on relationships, it is often possible to give the dynamics of finding meaning in dreams a direction that is sound from a traditional, a Christian, a moral and a psychological perspective.

Cultural concepts sometimes allow for an interpretation of a dream to be pulled into very different directions; interpretations are often contested. Uncomfortable dreams have often been used to accuse others of witchcraft. But this does not need to be the case. A Christian spirituality can give the whole process of seeking meaning in a dream a direction that leads towards action motivated by faith:

> **Dream: my dead child shows me the witch**
> *My baby died. I started to dream about the baby, nearly every night. I was dressing up the child or wrapping the child, because I wanted to go to Church. On my way to Church with the baby on my back I would meet our neighbour, standing and watching from afar. She was not saying anything, just standing and looking at us from a distance, uncomfortably. Then I woke up. This dream came back so many times. Then I asked a friend about the meaning. She said: "The baby wants to show you the witch who killed it. This woman has killed your child!" And it is true: after our child died and we had buried the child, somebody stole from the grave the dish which we had put there on the*

91

grave. We know that the child died through witchcraft. From then onwards I avoided my neighbour. We were good friends before. But now I started to think that she was a witch.

The Christian couple did not intend to visit a diviner to look for more proof; this would have contradicted the demands of their Christian faith. But the mother of the baby started to avoid her neighbour. The dreams, however, did not stop. In subsequent events it became clear that the neighbour at least had nothing to do with what had happened to the grave. The dish on the grave had been stolen by some youths on behalf of a visiting diviner, who needed something from a grave for preparing his medicines. The husband was very angry with the diviner and placed back the dish on the grave, without failing to express his anger. Subsequently he became more and more sceptical about the interpretation given to the wife. He came up with another way of looking at the dream:

Why should our neighbour be a witch? There was no motive for her to kill our child. The child was not showing us the murderer. But there is a reason why our neighbour was always in the dream: the child had her name. Our neighbour had given her own name to the child when it was born. In the dream my wife was always on the way to Church with the baby when she found our neighbour on the way, standing there, watching and not moving anywhere. The child was showing us whom to bring back to Church, because our neighbour had stopped praying. She had stopped singing in the choir since our child died. This was our task that was given to us in the dreams after our child died.

The husband's way of making sense of his wife's dream gave it a positive direction. Though his wife needed some time to warm up towards her husband's interpretation, she too agreed that it provided a better way and a Christian manner of responding to the dream in a way that builds up rather than destroys.

Bibliography

Baker, C. F. (1971). *A Dispensational Theology.* Michigan: Grace Bible College.

Domhoff, G. W. (2010). *The Case for a Cognitive Theory of Dreams.* Retrieved August 10, 2012 from the World Wide Web: http://dreamresearch.net/Library/domhoff_2010.html

Fabian, J. (1966). Dream and Charisma. 'Theories of Dreams' in the Jamaa Movement (Congo). *Anthropos, 61*(3), 544-560.

Freud, S. (1947 (1899)). *Die Traumdeutung.* Frankfurt am Main: Fischer Taschenbuch Verlag.

Hall, C. S. (1953). A cognitive theory of dreams. *The Journal of General Psychology, 49,* 273-282.

Jędrej, M. C., & Shaw, R. (1992). Introduction: Dreaming, Religion and Society in Africa. In M. C. Jędrej, & R. Shaw, *Dreaming, Religion and Society in Africa* (pp. 1-20). Leiden: Brill.

Johnson, R. A. (1989). *Inner Work: Using Dreams and Active Imagination for Personal Growth.* Harper & Harper.

Jones, J. W. (1991). The Relational Self: Contemporary Psychoanalysis Reconsiders Religion. *Journal of the American Academy of Religion, 59*(1), 119-134.

Kandel, E. (2005). *Psychiatry, psychoanalysis, and the new biology of mind.* Amer Psychiatric Pub.

Masamba Ma Mpolo, J., & Kalu, W. (1985). *The Risks of Growth. Counselling & Pastoral Theology in the African Context.* Nairobi: Uzima Press Ltd.

Mentzos, S. (2011). *Lehrbuch der Psychdynamik: Die Funktion der Dysfunktionalität psychischer Störungen.* Göttingen: Vandenhoeck & Ruprecht.

O'Hara. (1997). Relational Empathy: From Egocentrism to Postmodern Contextualism. In A. Bohardt, & L. Greenberg, *Empathy and Psychotherapy: New directions in theory, research and practice.* Washington, D.C.: American Psychological Association.

O'Hara, M. (n.d.). *Relational Empathy: Beyond Modernist Egocentrism to Postmodern Holistic Contextualisation.* Retrieved August 8, 2011, from the World Wide Web: http://maureen.ohara.net/pubs/Relational%20Empathy.pdf

Reynolds, P. (1992). Dreams and the Constitution of Self among the Zezeru. In M. Jędrej, & R. Shaw, *Dreaming, Religion and Society in Africa* (pp. 21-35). Leiden: Brill.

6

The Interpretation of my dream

Patrick Mumbi.

I want to reflect on one of my dreams which is open to very different aspects of interpretation, namely to psychodynamic and to transpersonal/spiritual ways. Let me begin by narrating the dream. I was asleep and I dreamt of going to South Africa where I had never been before, though deep down I had anxiously desired to go there. It seemed also in the dream that I had been there before, and now I was going back for the second time, without other people knowing about it, so it seemed. When I arrived, the place of the Parish house looked yellow-brownish and beautiful, but this might just be my own imagination of South Africa's surroundings.

As I arrived I saw the Parish priest through the window and he was eating something. I was feeling afraid that he was going to reprimand me for coming to South Africa again. But he welcomed me and mentioned my name saying, *"Patrick welcome"*. But then I did not enter the Parish house; instead I went to the shop near-by to buy a memory stick. I found many decorated ones with pinkish handles and there were many varieties of this type in that shop and I bought one. It seemed I was accompanied by another fellow whom I could not remember. As we went out of the shop we saw a friend of mine, a fellow priest, who was fighting with another man, and he was jumping up and down as they were fighting. We were on a certain tarred road where we saw this fight taking place. From there I woke up and that was the end of the dream.

In analysing this dream I fall back on what Freud said that a dream is divided in two aspects namely the manifest content and the latent content (Freud, 1995, 206). The manifest content is the part of the dream that we remember – the history lines, a facade of our dream according to Jung. If for example someone asked me to share about my dream, I could simply tell him or her that I was just dreaming about going to South Africa. The other aspect of the dream, according to Freud, is the latent content and it concerns the underlying, more hidden but true meaning of the dream. The latent content is censored or condensed by our unconscious or subconscious. The latent content also reflects the dream thought: a thought/ a wish, which becomes objectified in a dream and is represented as a scene or as we think or experience. But the representation is represented in the present. Dream thoughts (latent) are thoughts translated into visual images and speech entering into the dream content. Remember also that our life is spent in a struggle for the realisation of our wishes. All our actions proceed from a wish that something should happen.

Analysing my dream, I think I have been relishing a thought of going to South Africa, but I have never been offered a chance of going there. I have admired those who have been frequenting South Africa and have been jealous of them, though I have never talked about that openly. Jung on this could say, "*We imagine that which we lack*" (Jung, 1991, 28). Notice also that in the dream I had the feeling of fear, because I had again returned to South Africa and for that I felt that the Parish priest was going to reprimand me for doing so, but he did not. Looking again at the other part of the dream, as I arrived in the Parish in South Africa where I saw the Parish priest welcoming me, I did not enter the house but instead went to the shop to buy the memory stick. From the psychoanalytic experience, whenever one recounts his phantasies or his dreams, he/she not only deals with the most important and intimate of his/her problems, but with the one that is the most painful at that moment. This may be the loss of a beloved one, longing for good health, a breakdown etc. At that moment I was grieving for the loss of my two memory sticks which contained a lot of important academic material. I had rubbed off all the information from my computer and preserved everything on the memory stick, but only to lose everything. There was no way of retrieving the material, except to suffer the pain of loss wholeheartedly. I had searched all over my room to look for some papers pertaining to the above material, but I found only some rough drafts of the papers that I had printed. But this thought of losing exam material tormented me for months; it came back later in my dreams. Here it should be borne in mind that in waking life there are issues we cannot uncover, because they are frightening, painful and shaming. Therefore it is the purpose of psychoanalysis or counselling to help uncover the hidden meanings. There are many symbolisms in dreams that one cannot unearth publicly to anybody, though one can do so in counselling.

In one of our sessions after the conference on dreams, a woman narrated one of her frequent dreams. She said that she was married, but during the night she dreams of a man who comes to make love with her. But she does not know this man because she sees only the body and not the face of the man. Another woman who was having the same dream said that whenever she closes her house to go to bed, she sees a shadow of a person quickly entering her house. Upon opening the door, the following morning she again sees a shadow slipping out. She went to the priest to look for holy water which she sprinkled in her house to make this shadow disappear, so that she could sleep without being raped by this invisible figure.

Several interpretations can be ascribed to these repetitive dreams of the women. Some traditional healers said these dreams pertain to witchcraft. They explained that witches are very crafty people and can even use animals to represent themselves. Another traditional healer added that other witches use the tail of the hyena or fox (putting it between their buttocks) to conceal themselves and thereafter make love to the woman they admire, while others use herbs to conceal themselves and prey on their loved ones. But the surprising thing is that the woman cannot get pregnant no matter how many times she sleeps with this shadow man. In analysing this problem one may also reflect on the relationship that this woman has with her husband. If the relationship between them is strong and loving there is nothing that can come between them and these dreams will disappear. But if there are some constraints in the relationship and the woman seeks a relationship outside marriage, the man of her love can come in a dream.

Sometimes in our life we struggle or fight with our own shadows, desires, hateful feelings beneath our own consciousness. At other times we are not fully conscious of our own self and at other times we try to hide or show a wrong facade to others, but these things will appear in our dreams to torment us. Freud once said *"If our marriage-agent stories are witticisms at all, they are all the better witticisms because, thanks to their facade, they are in a position to conceal not only what they have to say but also that they have something forbidden to say"* (Freud, 1995, 668). What he says may shed some light on the above marriage constraints, namely that *"the marriage-agent (in the dream) is thus transformed from a ludicrous personage into an object deserving of pity and sympathy"* (p.668). We can see all images in our dreams/hallucinations especially if our (love) relationship we once cherished has gone bad.

Notice again the transpersonal /spiritual aspect of the dream. I have never been to South Africa, it is a fact, but through the dream I happened to be there. How? According to Freud and even Jung, since the dream is unconcerned with the real condition of things, it brings the most heterogeneous matter together and a world of impossibilities takes the place of realities (Jung, 1991, 23). Nietzsche pondered once if our dreams do not recapitulate the whole thought of earlier humanity in the way that how a person reasons in his/her dreams, humans reasoned when in the waking state many thousands of years. Through the dream we can connect and reach the world we have never been to, meet our forefathers and our ancestors of long ago. We can even reach the future world where our ancestors have gone before us. According to Jung the unconscious contains within it not only the possibilities of decomposition to the primitive but also the seeds of our highest evolutionary capacities. Jung also saw the myth of the human race as wish fulfilling the prophecies recapitulating the entire evolutionary psychic life of the species (Jung, 1991, xxii-xxiii).

A friend of mine narrated to me a dream that he had when he was sick. In it he entered a very dark space and wanted to reach somewhere. But then he saw a dark figure which prevented him from going and they began to fight. Unfortunately, the figure overcame him and threw him to the ground. Then he was lifted upside down, his head dangling. But then there came a rope which lowered him down. He thought that he had entered hell. But then he remembered having a conversation with one of the priests that hell is the absence of love. But in his life he had loved parents, father, mother and brothers and sisters; so he said to himself, *"Ah I can transform hell into love because I have loved all these people close to me".* Surprisingly a smell came to his nostrils and it was a smell of tobacco which his grandmother was using together with her perfume. This helped him to get alive and he was able to find his way and enter the dark side which opened up for him. He was able to see his ancestors, namely his forefathers and grandfathers and mothers. Here again we come across Jung's archetype motives and mythological figures. In his sort of lucid dream he managed to synthesise Christian elements with his traditional cultural aspect of life but at the same time showed commitment to both of them. Maybe deep down in his life, there was a loss of or a disconnection with his ancestors. Others may call this struggle for full identity which many of us have lost in this modern world of individualism, globalisation and materialism. We have become isolated from our life-lines and become little islands, but only a problem needs to come and it will haunt us some day. The motif of the dark environment or the black figure may reflect the dark side of ourselves which we may not like. I remember the song we used to sing: *"will you bring the you, you hide in you when I but call your name".* Maybe if we come to accept or know the 'you' or the 'me' that I or we hide about ourselves, our life would be empowered. But very often we try not even to talk about this and we get angry when others begin to get close to this "you" we hide in ourselves.

Therefore, dreams could reveal a true nature of ourselves and enlarge our consciousness. Furthermore, they can connect us to the rest of humanity, dead or living, future, all of nature, and renew our life (Welling, 2004, 17). Through the dream, we can go beyond the usual limits of consciousness, with the individual self finally dissolving (p.187).

Bibliography

Jung, Carl C. (1991). *Psychology of the unconscious. A study of the transformations and symbolisms of the Libido*. Princeton: Princeton University Press

Sigmund F. (1995ed). *The Basic Writings of Sigmund Freud. Psycho-pathology of everyday life. The Interpretation of Dreams*. New York: The modern Library

Welling N & Wilde E. (2004).*Transpersonal Psychotherapy, Theory and Practice*. London: Sage Publication.

7

A questionnaire to help detecting the meaning of your dreams

Gotthard Rosner

This questionnaire is inspired by the book of George R. Slater (1995). Bringing Dreams to Life: Learning to interpret your Dreams. *Paulist Press, New York 1995.*

The setting

The setting (place, building, landscape...) of a dream might give a first indication of the meaning of the dream.

E.g. *I was walking in a dark forest...* might point out a problem in life.

I was in our living room at home... might point towards a wrong relationship in the family.

The setting might also refer to events which happened in the recent past or in childhood.

The images

What are the images or symbols which occurred in the dream (objects, persons, animals, rain, dancing, funeral, mountain...)?

What meaning have these symbols in our culture (past and present)?

- e.g. a snake: In the past sign of blessings coming from an ancestor; today sign of a demon or of the danger coming from witchcraft.

- A lion: a symbol of strength or of a new energy, the symbol of an ancestor or the symbol of danger and death.

What do these symbols or images mean to me personally?

The images of a dream represent life-forces or energies, good or evil ones.

The main theme of the dream

What story happened in the dream? Are there more than one story or actions? Does the dream point towards relationships with people (relationships with family members, with the community, with the ancestors)?

The effect of the story when dreaming

Was there any suggestion for a change in life, a resolution or a problem solved in the dream itself? What energy or life-force was flowing or blocked in the dream?

- A fire might point towards some new life-energy needed.

- The visit of a deceased husband might point out a problem in the extended family.

- A new-born child often signifies a new beginning.

Feelings when dreaming

What emotions did you experience when dreaming (joy, fear, wonder, horror...)? What are the values experienced in the dream?

The context

a. The feelings when waking up

Was there a sense of relief, when the dream was frightening? Were there different feelings present in the dream and when waking up?

A dream might represent the challenge to accept new contents into consciousness (personal and social).

b. Previous day's events and future events

"Freud believed that dreams responded to the previous day's events. Jung, while not so narrowly focused, regarded dreams as the dialogue which the unconscious carries on with the conscious mind, usually in the light of recent events." (G. Slater, Dreams, p.85).

Events of the near future might also be shown in a dream. E.g. dreaming of a funeral or a coffin might point towards the death of a loved one. Dreaming of Jesus might urge somebody to begin a more spiritual life or to follow a special call. Dreaming to be with a loved person might show the arrival of this person in the near future or the support received by this person.

c. The emotional state of the dreamer in life.

It is important to consider the emotional state of a person prior to the dream. Was the person under stress, upset or in great difficulties? Is the person at peace or are there worries and problems?

Associations

What comes to mind when I think of or relive the dream?

These associations might appear unreasonable or absurd, but those "stray thoughts" might connect you to life.

A desert or sand evokes dryness or the absence of life. Green grass might signify plenty of food or a high living standard. A mountain might be associated with the feeling of freedom or being close to God.

What in your life is similar to the elements of the dream? What memories does the dream bring back? (connect to your life-story).

Amplifications

We might be able to expand the message or symbols of a dream. Symbols always hide the reality. They need to be drawn out or amplified.

a. Balance

How is your dream different concerning your attitudes or values when being awake? The images might point towards a potential personal growth or towards reconciliation with other persons. Our structured way of life might open up to new possibilities.

b. Active imagination

When fully awake, relive the dream and begin a dialogue with the different persons or images of the dream. New insights might be won.

c. Confronting a monster

To face the "monster" (a horrifying person) of your dream might present the opportunity of coming to terms with deep personal fears. Facing the monster in active imagination might bring transformation. Giving the monster a friendly name, asking for its origin and purpose and asking to be your friend might have amazing results.

Questions and Answers

What questions of my life are answered in the dream? Does the dream give me some new knowledge? What does it tell me about myself and others? If the dream is disturbing, what would help to find peace?

A QUSTIONNAIRE

Give yourself plenty of time to discover, explore and find the message of a dream.

Gotthard Rosner

About the authors

Gotthard Rosner holds an MA in Divinity (Ottawa University), an MA in Theology (St. Paul's University, Ottawa) and a Licentiate of the Biblical Institute in Rome. As a missionary he worked in Uganda, Zambia, France and Italy. He has been teaching in Gulu (Uganda), Lusaka and Kasama (Zambia) and in the Catholic Institute in Toulouse. From 1992 to 1998 he held the position of Superior General of the Missionaries of Africa. Since then he has been working for on-going formation programmes for Diocesan priests in Zambia. Presently he is the director of the Faith and Encounter Centre Zambia (FENZA). In Zambia he has published several Biblical works together with the Zambian Episcopal Conference. He has been a regular contributor to various Christian magazines.

Bernhard Udelhoven holds an STB in theology (Leuven) and an MA in social anthropology (SOAS, University of London). In Zambia, he has been working since 1989 in the Luapula, Eastern and Lusaka provinces. Some of his publications on Zambian Christianity, on the Luangwa Valley, on witchcraft and Satanism, culture change, and on healing are available on the FENZA website (fenza.org/documents).

Patrick Mumbi holds a PhD in cultural studies from Makerere University (Uganda), an MA in social anthropology from SOAS (University of London), and a MA in counselling from University of East-Anglia. He has written about incest and child sexual abuse (Uganda), about Bemba psychotherapy in the cross-cultural setting (Zambia), and on Christian inculturation of twin ceremonies (Uganda). At present he is working on a research project with traditional healers in Lusaka. A forthcoming book "Inheritance the end of moaning and mowing" is dealing with cultural values and family responsibilities that are part of the Bemba funeral rites.

The authors are members of the Missionaries of Africa and work presently for FENZA.

www.ingramcontent.com/pod-product-compliance
Lightning Source LLC
Chambersburg PA
CBHW070540290526
45790CB00002B/578